# The Bloke's Guide
# to Baby Gadgets

# The Bloke's Guide to Baby Gadgets

Jon Smith

HAY HOUSE

Australia • Canada • Hong Kong
South Africa • United Kingdom • United States

**First published and distributed in the United Kingdom by:**
Hay House UK Ltd, 292B Kensal Rd, London W10 5BE.
Tel.: (44) 20 8962 1230; Fax: (44) 20 8962 1239. www.hayhouse.co.uk

**Published and distributed in the United States of America by:**
Hay House, Inc., PO Box 5100, Carlsbad, CA 92018-5100.
Tel.: (1) 760 431 7695 or (800) 654 5126;
Fax: (1) 760 431 6948 or (800) 650 5115. www.hayhouse.com

**Published and distributed in Australia by:**
Hay House Australia Ltd, 18/36 Ralph St, Alexandria NSW 2015.
Tel.: (61) 2 9669 4299; Fax: (61) 2 9669 4144. www.hayhouse.com.au

**Published and distributed in the Republic of South Africa by:**
Hay House SA (Pty), Ltd, PO Box 990, Witkoppen 2068.
Tel./Fax: (27) 11 706 6612. orders@psdprom.co.za

**Distributed in Canada by:**
Raincoast, 9050 Shaughnessy St, Vancouver, BC V6P 6E5.
Tel.: (1) 604 323 7100; Fax: (1) 604 323 2600

The author of this book does not dispense medical advice or prescribe the
use of any technique as a form of treatment for physical or medical problems
without the advice of a physician, either directly or indirectly. The intent of
the author is only to offer information of a general nature to help you in
your quest for emotional and spiritual wellbeing. In the event you use any of
the information in this book for yourself, which is your constitutional right,
the author and the publisher assume no responsibility for your actions.

A catalogue record for this book is available from the British Library.

ISBN 1-4019-1166-8
ISBN 978-1-4019-1166-9

Design and layout by e-Digital Design.
Illustrations by Matt Windsor.
Printed and bound in Europe by Imago.

For Alia and Ronin

# Contents

## About the Author

Jon Smith is married with two children. He writes books, screenplays and musical theatre.

## Contact the Author

By post:
c/o Hay House
292B Kensal Road
London
W10 5BE
United Kingdom

By E-mail:
jon@blokesguide.com

On the Web:
http://www.jonsmith.net
http://www.justdads.co.uk

# Introduction

Well done, Sir. You came up with the goods all those weeks ago. There were some who doubted you, some who feared you'd abandon the mission, but you stuck to the plan and got the result. The battalion is proud of you. Your country is proud of you. The government is proud of you. Damn it, man, I don't say this often, but even I'm proud of you. Baby is developing well, Mother is doing fine and very soon you're going to be a dad! It's great news. You've even been allowed out a few times to enjoy a swift half with the boys to celebrate the forthcoming arrival, but beware: you have only won the battle, not the war.

Just when you thought it was safe to resume Tuesday nights in the *Wellington Arms*, it's time to shop until you drop. You knew it yourself, and in case you didn't, there have been some subtle hints left around the house that you couldn't possibly miss, like the note, 'Buy a sterilizer today at lunch or I'm leaving you for Dave from Accounts.'

Your background has taught you that preparation is key. The informed soldier is the soldier who survives to tell the tale. You might, of course, be a bit confused and actually have a background in the Scouts rather than the Royal Marines, but either way, you are prepared, and that's why you will go shopping with your head held high. The amount of stuff needed for a new baby is mind-boggling. Some of the price tags associated with said apparatus are absolutely criminal, but you'll still buy it. You'll still compare what other dads have and more importantly don't have when you pass each other on the high street. As you well know, the days of flashy two-seater sports cars ended pretty much as soon as junior's conception was announced, but something has to fill the place of that competitive style accessory. Something else will become the sole focus of your fixation with performance-related statistics, the thing you aim for, aspire to, save up for and put on wish lists at Christmas and for birthdays. Yes, it's Baby Gadgets. Bits and bobs that *you* just simply have to have, *and* you've got the fail-proof excuse that they're really for Baby, not you.

Never mind that our fathers and our father's fathers got by fine without any of this clobber, never mind that. Those lazy sods didn't change a single nappy. Who are they to tell you that their grandchild, *your child*, should be denied the best that life can give? Your new mission, Sir, is to seek as much intelligence as you can, plan your purchases and boldly go into the hostile and dangerous world of Baby Gadgets. It won't be easy, nor will it be cheap, but by God, man, we'll make it fun.

Do it for your child, do it for yourself. *Just Do It*.

# Gadgets for Mums Only

Throughout this book I have made the assumption that you, the dad, are happy to take an active interest in the bringing up of your child and therefore you will also be doing your fair share of the cooking, cleaning and all the other jobs that are traditionally associated with women. That said, there are some gadgets and products that are suitable only for mums, and there's no point pretending that Dad can have a go, or needs or in any ways gets to try to use these items. That's why Mum gets her own section. Everything else in this book is primarily aimed at Baby, but I also hope can be appreciated by Dad.

Right, you better get shopping, young man, because some of this stuff is going to be needed really soon, if not already. Off you go!

## Infant Cushion / Feeding Cushion

**Description:** There's no denying the fact that this really is just a very large sausage-shaped pillow or, depending on how much money is invested, a very large strip of foam, but just because a product is simple does not mean that it is any less valuable than one that's complicated and expensive. The infant cushion is a Ronseal gadget – it does exactly what it says on the tin. It's a cushion on which your partner can rest the bump while in bed or resting on the sofa during those final weeks of pregnancy, or that can be placed in between her legs for a more comfortable night's sleep. Once the baby is born the cushion doubles as a support for breast-feeding.

**Pros:** No matter how professional and competent your lady might look, right from day one bear in mind that breast-feeding is not that easy for most mums. The physical and emotional weight of a newborn baby feeding from your partner's boobs can be as daunting an experience for her as for you. Along with the psychological pressure of trying to get it right, there's the none-too-easy task of getting baby to 'latch' properly. A feeding cushion ensures that both Mum and Baby are comfortable during the feed, especially when you bear in mind that her first efforts will probably be in front of an audience – consisting of you and a midwife, at bare minimum. All this just a matter of minutes or hours after giving birth! Talk about pressure – and you find it difficult to wee in a busy urinal. You don't know you're born, mate.

**Cons:** None. That is, until the feeding cushion becomes an essential carry-everywhere item for your partner – a bit cumbersome when you first venture out to the Chinese restaurant as new parents, with child and cushion in tow.

**What's it all about?** The great thing about a feeding cushion is that they're really useful both before and after birth. Not only are they a comfort and a help for Mum, but on the occasions when Baby makes it into your bed, the foam wedge can be employed to form a barrier between Baby and the side of the bed. What's that you say? There's not enough room for you in the bed as well? Sorry, pal, off to the sofa with you.

**Bloke's Rating:** A girl – or a boy – can't have enough oversized cushions in the house. Worth buying even if you only use it to get comfortable in front of the television.

## Nursing Bras

**Description:** Best to leave buying this one to the girls, unless you are dispatched to John Lewis with the exact measurements, a floor map, drawings or cut-outs from magazines and solid assurance in the form of a signed contract that should you, for some unforeseeable reason, end up buying the wrong item or the wrong size, you will not be shouted at. Nursing bras are very expensive for what appears to be a straightforward enough item of clothing. Be warned that they are quite bizarre-looking: on first glance they could be mistaken for a kinky little S&M number, but they're not. They're a pragmatic solution offering your partner support whilst at the same time allowing her to whip her whups out at a moment's notice.

**Pros:** Weeks before your partner is actually nursing, she is going to have moved up a cup size or two in the boob department. You and she are both probably over the moon about the big and bouncy look, but believe it or not that extra size is not just for your amusement. Your partner's breasts will soon have a very important job to do – providing milk for your baby. What's great about a nursing bra is the flap feature, which means Mum can feed Baby without having to completely remove her underwear every time Baby wants a snack.

**Cons:** Other than being dreadfully unattractive, there's nothing really wrong with nursing bras, and now, for the trendy or ironic amongst you, there are even leopard-print versions available.

**What's it all about?** Along with buying a couple of nursing bras you will also get top marks if you come home with a couple of packs of breast pads – you can choose machine-washable or disposable versions – which help soak up any leaks, protecting your partner's clothes. They'll save her from the embarrassment of tell-tale wet patches.

**Bloke's Rating:** An essential for every mum's top drawer.

## Ultrasonic Doppler

**Description:** Also known as a Parental Heart Listening Device, which is slightly misleading because I am sure that the purpose is to listen to the heart beat of your unborn infant rather than Mum- and Dad-to-be playing doctors and nurses and getting up to all sorts of hanky-panky; but each to their own. The doppler is an entry-level version of what the professionals use in hospital and will allow you and Mum to listen to Baby's heart whenever you want.

**Pros:** Gone are the days when you have to wait weeks in between scans and appointments for any audio-visual contact with your baby – the doppler gives you the option to hear your baby and to allow friends and family the opportunity to listen in too. Some models come with two sets of head-phones, but you can use the built-in speaker too.

**Cons:** Other than the cost, having your own ultrasonic doppler is pretty cool. The special gel you will need to use is extra, but what price can you put on the absolutely fascinating experience of listening to your baby? On the flip side, detecting a baby's heartbeat accurately every time is an acquired art form and many a user has freaked-out when they are unable to hear any heart activity at all. Reposition the doppler and try again. Having a doppler can also mean Mum and/or Dad become quite obsessive about listening in on Junior. Remember, he needs his private time too!

**What's it all about?** For many parents-to-be the doppler offers peace of mind during what can feel like the wilderness of pregnancy. Dinner parties take on a whole new dimension when you pull out a doppler instead of offering your guests a brandy and a quick game of Trivial Pursuit.

**Bloke's Rating:** Kudos guaranteed.

# TENS machine

**Description:** A TENS machine is very similar to those contraptions that you can buy from infomercials on the less-well-known satellite channels and which offer a flatter stomach in four days if you just plug yourself in while watching a DVD and tucking into a doner kebab. The TENS pads are placed at strategic points on the lower back during labour and the small electrical pulses will stimulate your partner's body into producing natural painkillers known as endorphins. If your wife is planning a 'natural' birth and would rather not take any medical painkillers such as pethedine or an epidural, then the TENS machine – and entonox, or gas and air – will be the only choice left open to her other than giving birth without any assistance whatsoever.

**Pros:** Some TENS users swear that the experience lessened the pain of the early contractions during labour. As the pain of the contractions grows, the TENS machine can be adjusted to a higher level offering the user a stronger pulse so they'll produce more endorphins. It is possible to give birth while wearing a TENS machine, but most users remove the pads once contractions are in full force because no battery-powered device is going to help reduce the excruciating pain of actually giving birth. TENS machines are reasonably cheap to buy or hire, and it is possible to just borrow one from the hospital when labour is occurring, although there is no guarantee they will have any when your partner needs it. In defence of the TENS machine, whether the pulses are helping or not, the whole process of putting the pads on your partner and adjusting the levels can prove to be a welcome distraction during the early stages of labour.

**Cons:** I gave the TENS machine a cutting review in my book *The Bloke's Guide to Pregnancy* and I haven't altered my opinion since Lisa gave birth to our second child, Ronin. It's rather telling that Lisa chose not to bother with a TENS machine at all the second time round. Some mums-to-be find all the cables and pads become annoying as they try to alter their position during labour – bear in mind that your partner will probably be wired up to the foetal heart monitor and have a tube and mouthpiece for the entonox, and that's more than enough to get tangled up in.

**What's it all about?** It's very easy to have an opinion, but as I never have given and never will give birth, I honestly can't say whether TENS machines are any good. However, after seeing my wife throw hers across the room during her first labour, my money is on 'don't bother'.

**Bloke's Rating:** It's up to your partner.

## Inflatable Birthing Pool

**Description:** An oversized paddling pool for your home. Usually circular or oval in shape, the pool comes with strategic handles for Mum to grip and, unlike a child's paddling pool, the sides are deep enough to give the capacity and space for Mum to manoeuvre around while still being semi-submerged in the water and remaining buoyant. Yes, it is big enough for Dad to have a go, but it's best not to jump in at the same time as your pregnant partner!

**Pros:** Water births are heralded as the most natural and least painful way to endure labour and give birth. Many hospitals now offer birthing pools, but it's often pot luck if one happens to be free at the time that your baby has decided to put in an appearance. For many couples, a home birth is the preferred location for delivery and so the Inflatable Birthing Pool offers the chance of a guaranteed water birth in the comfort of your own home. Far cheaper than the 'professional' pools that can be bought or hired, and you don't have to worry about having the baby before the lease runs out.

**Cons:** Buy an air pump! Don't even contemplate blowing the thing up manually. Water is very heavy and therefore you need to erect the pool in the room in which your partner is going to give birth; and bring the water to the pool, not the other way round. Make sure you have a few buckets in the house – dragging the garden hose through the house might seem like a good idea but your partner will soon tell you what she thinks of the cold water.

**What's it all about?** Water births are good for Mum and for Baby and now you have the affordable option to do it at home. If this is what your partner wants, this is what you should hire or buy.

**Bloke's Rating:** Brilliant.

## Caesarean Belt

**Description:** For any mum who has already or will soon undergo a Caesarean through choice or necessity, not only has she got to cope with the shock of dealing with a new baby, but her body has to recover from the trauma of major surgery. The Caesarean belt is placed around the wound and offers support, protection and, with the additional hot and cold pads, can give some gentle relief from the pain or itchiness she experiences as the body heals.

**Pros:** Whenever we injure ourselves, be it just a cut on a finger or a bruised arm, it is staggering how many times we bang the sore area throughout the day. A Caesarean scar is no different and the belt offers added protection from any accidental knocks.

**Cons:** A Caesarean belt will not speed up the healing process and it remains your responsibility to ensure that your partner is still resting when she can and not trying to take on too much too soon.

**What's it all about?** Even when 'taking it easy', Mum will be bending, lifting, sitting and walking – each of those movements will be using abdominal muscles and will therefore be painful for many weeks after surgery. The Caesarean belt really helps.

**Bloke's Rating:** A post-surgery must.

## Breast Pump / Extractor

**Description:** A breast pump is for mums who want to feed their baby breast milk but may not be close by to baby at feeding time, due to work or social commitments. The breast pump allows Mum to extract breast milk for baby to take at a later date. Your partner will place the suction cup over the nipple area of her breast, the cup forms an airtight seal and operating the pump causes a vacuum and assists your partner in expressing her milk. The milk is collected in a container – usually a bottle – which can easily be sealed with a lid. There are manual pumps and electric pumps. The manual versions have a handle to squeeze to keep the vacuum going and thus keep the milk flowing. The electric versions are much more 'plug-and-play'.

**Pros:** For us dads it's pretty hard to get a look-in at dinner time when your partner is breastfeeding. While we will all agree that breast is best, it can cause stirs of jealousy seeing your newborn derive so much pleasure from Mum while you're sitting watching like a lemon. Suddenly your partner declares she is going out on Saturday for an afternoon of lavish shopping and indulgence. Hurrah! She expresses, goes off with the credit card and you're left holding the baby and some lukewarm breast milk. Brilliant.

Another benefit for mums is the ability to express when their breasts are feeling sore and engorged. Sometimes Baby doesn't take a full feed, but more and more milk is being produced – this can be incredibly uncomfortable. Having a breast pump in the house can relieve the pressure.

**Cons:** Manual breast pumps can take ages to do the job, and while there's no pain involved – the experience should feel the same as when a baby suckles – it can be pretty boring for Mum. Although the electric pumps are far faster, and some would argue far more thorough, there is the associated higher price. If, however, this is a path your partner is seriously considering, then it is well worth talking to a breastfeeding counsellor or the local NCT about hiring one. Try before you buy.

**What's it all about?** If your partner is going to be working, then the electric pump is the boy for the job. If, however, your partner is only planning to be out without the baby for an hour or two every now and again, then the manual pump makes far more sense.

**Bloke's Rating:** Feeding Baby is a great experience. Encourage your partner to go out as much as possible, leaving you to look after and feed the baby. She gets some well-deserved space to herself and you get that all-important quality time with your newborn.

## Nipple Shields

**Description:** Pieces of silicone that are placed over the nipples and allow Baby to continue breastfeeding but offer protection if your partner's nipples are sore or chapped. They also give Baby something to latch onto if the nipples are inverted or flat.

**Pros:** Breastfeeding, although natural, is not always straightforward for Baby or for Mum. Nipple shields can be the compromise that mums who are having difficulty or who are in pain are looking for: it allows them to continue feeding and not to have to resort to formula milk.

**Cons:** The baby sucks the milk through the shield rather than from the nipple direct, and some mums feel like they have failed. This is not the case at all. The important thing is that Baby is getting natural breast milk whenever he wants and the fact that a bit of silicone is helping that process is absolutely irrelevant.

**What's it all about?** Breastfeeding is often an emotive subject. Anything that helps promote natural milk should be applauded, though perhaps your partner should try using ointments first if she is suffering from cracked or sore nipples. Kamilosan is a firm favourite with most mums. If the problems persist then it is advisable she contacts a breastfeeding counsellor.

**Bloke's Rating:** Worth giving them a go, if all else fails.

# Communications

For the vast majority of time your newborn baby will be attached either to the breast of your partner or to the teat of a feeding bottle, or he'll be asleep. Either way, he or she will be in the hands – literally – of either you or your partner, or tucked up in the little basket right there in front of you both, sucking on his lip and epitomising the words cute, cuddly and perfect. The weeks will pass – rather too quickly – and suddenly you'll be measuring time as a matter of months rather than days and a schedule will appear. Baby sleeps, Baby wakes, Baby feeds, Baby plays, Baby cries. Repeat.

As your baby becomes more accustomed to the intricacies of life on the outside, there comes the time, believe it or not, when you have to put him down to sleep in a room you are not occupying. He might spend an hour or two every now and again with his grandparents or, perish the thought, he might be asleep upstairs, allowing you and your partner a brief taste of time alone together downstairs without a child. Imagine that – a bit of peace and quiet and the now strange opportunity to put on a DVD with the best intentions, before the two of you promptly fall asleep on the sofa. This is life with a baby. You'll love it. I promise.

But with the removal of constant 24/7 contact comes the inevitable feeling of fear. This poor little mite can't possibly survive without Mum and Dad – even if said parents are only on the other side of a plasterboard wall. How can we know that Junior is really OK as he sleeps in his cot, or spends the night with grandparents, or, horror of horrors, alone in the house with a mobile-phone-mad teenage babysitter who is far more preoccupied with wondering whether Carl will text back within the prescribed five minutes than whether Junior might be clutching onto life upstairs.

We can be a paranoid lot, us parents, and there's nothing wrong with that. Thankfully, to keep the economy ticking over, keep our hands in our pockets and to give us a sense of security, there is a wonderful array of products on the market that ensure that Baby can remain safe and sound in the veritable minefield of pain and misery that can be the modern 21st-century home.

## Baby Monitor

**Description:** A listening device not dissimilar to those walkie-talkies we all had as kids. The base unit is usually static and either plugs into the power socket in the wall or takes batteries. The parental unit is usually battery-powered which means you can carry it around the house with you, along with your cordless landline, mobile phone, MP3 player and your PDA – isn't technology just great? If your baby cries, or whimpers, or just breathes heavily – should the gadget be particularly sensitive – you will hear the sound through the monitor.

**Pros:** Very young babies make the strangest cacophony of noises during the first few months. Their breathing can seem erratic, noisy, sniffled and guttural, all in the space of just five minutes. As a new parent these unfamiliar sounds can be alarming and a constant source of worry. By using a monitor, many parents feel more comfortable leaving their baby alone in a different room, while they get on with other things. Be aware that it can be very exciting when a police car drives past using the same radio frequency – you tend to get one side of their radio conversation, and Baby wakes up to the sound of a hot pursuit.

**Cons:** We've lived in a big house and a small house with young babies and there hasn't once been an occasion where we haven't heard a baby wail – there's something so unique and penetrating about the sound of crying that as a parent you just can't ignore it, no matter how loud the television or how many closed doors are in between you and the sleeping infant. Bear in mind that baby monitors will not fix whatever is causing your baby to cry and they are not a substitute for investigating what is wrong with the bambino. Be sure to buy a monitor that has a choice of channels, otherwise you are likely to hear the cries of every other child on the block other than your own.

**What's it all about?** Having a baby monitor is all about peace of mind. There is something reassuring about hearing a groan or a moan or a cough coming through the monitor every now and again as you both sit down to watch *EastEnders*. If you spend a lot of time in the garden during the day, then there is a good reason to install a monitor in the baby's room – some of them have an enormous 400m range, which is probably a bit excessive.

**Bloke's Rating:** It's very difficult not to buy a monitor with your first child, but don't break the bank.

## TV Baby Monitor

**Description:** This is baby monitoring for the digital age – a small camera in the cot, linked to a receiver elsewhere. Not only do you receive audio of your child's wails of anguish, but you can also watch the little cherub from the comfort of your own sofa – right there on your super-slim LCD flat-screen. That's right. Plug this bad boy into your AV input and channel O becomes *Baby TV*.

**Pros:** There are occasions when babies have a little cry before falling into a deep, long sleep. As a parent it's often a toss-up between letting your baby cry and eventually fall asleep, or running upstairs to check everything is OK, thus exciting the baby and prolonging the crying. With visual access to your baby through the camera, parents can know whether their baby is crying because his leg is stuck between the bars of the cot, or whether he's just having a moan because he's really tired.

**Cons:** A lot like *Big Brother* – nothing happens when you're watching and the moment you turn the telly off and go to bed it's all action.

**What's it all about?** As far as impressing friends and family goes, the TV monitor is definitely a winner; they're expensive, funky and very cutting-edge – but it does beg the question of how we all managed to cope for all these years without one? The answer: quite easily.

**Bloke's Rating:** This is a cruel game of manipulation by the manufacturers. Trust in your own ability as parents.

## Cordless phone

**Description:** Juggling your responsibilities to the newborn with maintaining contact with the outside world is easier with a cordless. The phone rings, and, if you're sensible, the handset is right beside you on the sofa along with your mobile, and a change of nappy. Mind you, it's more likely to be in the other room, right where you left it a few hours ago.

**Pros:** If you're willing to carry the handset around with you – you slave to technology – you'll never miss a call or be caught out. Minimum effort, maximum return – the lazy way of always being available.

**Cons:** Your understanding of life will narrow to the idea that without your mobile in your right hand and your landline in your left, you are incomplete as a human being. You will become obsessed with batteries and power retention. You'll begin to get psychosomatic side effects when your phone battery is running low. You'll even start taking calls, or worse, *initiating* calls when you're on the loo. You sick puppy.

**What's it all about?** Jokes aside, your child can and will wrap the cord of a regular telephone around his or her neck. There is nothing fun about a child turning blue, and strangulation can easily be avoided by purchasing a wireless telephone. They look flash, they're all the rage and they save lives. It's time to update your telephone system.

# Mobility

'Best of luck, I'll just show you all to the door.'
'Yes, but what do we do when...'
'Bye!'

What? That's it?! No manual? No escort to the car to check you are doing everything right? No forms to sign and no fee to be paid? What a strange, strange feeling. The long walk out of the hospital door with a newborn baby into the big bad world is about as terrifying as the birth itself. Why is everything so noisy? Who are these people smoking in the car park? Get away from my pure, innocent, healthy child, you sick, slipper-wearing freak! Don't you dare reach out to touch my child with your unwashed, filth-ridden hands of death. Show some bloody respect!

Then there's a small altercation with the baby seat and some confusion over just *how* it fits into the car, now that it's occupied. As the sweat beads begin to form on your brow, finally there's a resounding click of success. Fumbling in your pockets for change, thankfully for the last time in a while, you are free of the hospital car park and away. As you cruise along at a deft 10mph, the streets have never felt so dangerous. A quick glance in the rear-view mirror reveals a tiny little body fast asleep and rocking violently to every bump in the far-from-satisfactory road on which you are driving. You might only have a twenty-minute drive to get home, but it feels like hours and the sense of relief at safely arriving outside the house is almost orgasmic. Your body is screaming for a stiff Scotch, to steady the nerves; the brain is telling you not to touch a drop. This is not funny in the slightest.

Slowly but surely you guide your war-worn partner gently into the house, supporting her every step of the way. The birth you have so recently witnessed is still very much in your mind's eye: only a matter of hours ago a new life entered the world and you witnessed it all. If it wasn't for the baby seat and your bad knee, you'd be offering to carry your partner straight up to bed and insist she rest for a couple of months. Then, unexpectedly, the pain kicks in. Why is it that your little bundle of joy, the one lying so quietly in the baby seat you're clutching, suddenly weighs as much as a bag of cement? If you don't get in the house pretty sharpish, the weight is likely to rip your arm out of its socket. Eight pounds two ounces, my arse!

I'm not just trying to scare you, that's how it is. You'll want to spend a bit of time deciding which forms of transport you are going to purchase for the little one. There are so many options that it can all be a bit baffling, but hopefully this chapter will take you through the high points, the low points, the pros and the cons.

Try as you might to protect your little newborn in the cotton-wool world of your home, there will come a time when you will need to take your baby out. To the shops for instance, or to see relatives and friends, but mainly to stop yourself and Baby getting cabin fever. You need to look at buying car seats, a pram, a pushchair and a whole assortment of products that will allow you or your partner to carry your progeny on your chest or on your back – and in a few months time, maybe a little plastic or wooden vehicle just for Baby.

## Car Seat – with Carry Handle

**Description:** Baby seats come in a wonderful array of shapes, colours and sizes. You can spend anywhere from £100 to £500-plus on a car seat but they do all boil down to pretty much the same thing. For newborns through to about nine months, or 10kg, you will need a rear-facing seat with its own buckle system to contain the baby, and then the seat itself is secured in the car using the seat belt. The varying prices appear to be based on how much filling goes into the upholstery, how many subtle positions the chair can be moved into, the chunkiness of the carry handle and the 'funkiness' of the pattern printed on the chair.

**Pros:** Life with a car seat means you can be mobile with your baby whether you are visiting family and friends or simply going shopping. There will be occasions when you load up your baby and simply drive around the block a few times to get her to go to sleep. The benefit of the car seat is that you can pull out the handle and carry your sleeping infant from the car to wherever you are going next without disturbing them. As the carry seats are mobile by definition, you can transfer your child easily from car to car knowing that they are safe.

**Cons:** There are no cons to car seats: they are absolutely essential if you want to transport a baby in a car. Unfortunately, each car seat will come with a unique and at first apparently impossible-to-decipher guide to installation. If you buy your car seat from one of the larger retailers and actually from a shop rather than online, the chances are you will be able to insist a sales assistant shows you how to fit it. Bear in mind that you can practise as much as you like before Baby comes along, but it's a whole lot tougher once Baby is actually sitting in the chair.

**What's it all about?** As a minimum you will want to buy a seat that can be adjusted from sitting position to reclining. Sitting is obviously great, allowing baby to see around him and be stimulated or possibly just terrified by everything that is rushing past outside. The reclining position is fantastic when a bit of quiet time is required, or when you've just overspent at Ikea – again – and you need to fit loads of flat-pack furniture into the foot-well underneath Baby.

**Bloke's Rating:** Buy what you can afford. Baby car seats are pretty robust and, therefore, no doubt the one you buy now will do for any future kids you may decide to have.

## Fixed Car Seat – the Early Years

**Description:** The oh-how-you've-grown stage is no more apparent than when you need to upgrade Baby's first car seat. No sooner have you mastered the 'carry-everywhere' car seat than you'll need to buy another one. Your little baby is not so little any more and no longer fits into that teeny-tiny seat that just a few months ago seemed to envelop her. How can just breast milk cause such growth?

**Pros:** Your first fixed car seat suddenly alters the layout and look of your car. It's your little statement to the world that you are a father and you're proud of the way you've had to customise the back seat. The new fixed car seat will be front-facing, have recline options and may even be available in exciting animal print designs. Yes, it's time to pimp Baby's ride.

**Cons:** This car seat will have a limited lifespan. It'll take you from the nine-to-twelve-month mark through to about three years.

**What's it all about?** Your baby is big enough and aware enough to want to look out of the windows. You're also beyond the point now where the simple act of placing a baby in the car results in hours of peaceful and unbroken sleep. Baby wants to look and feel important and the fixed car seat is without a doubt the answer.

**Bloke's Rating:** Well, it lasts a little longer than the carry car seat. For small mercies you should be thankful.

## Travel/Booster Seats

**Description:** Kids continue to grow at a remarkable rate – you'll know this already because some of the 0–3-month stuff you and your family bought for your newborn baby wasn't even out of the packet or off the hanger before your son or daughter was into the next size. The same happens to the car seats. Just as you'd got inserting and extracting Baby's car seat down to a fine art, or just after you have installed her first fixed car seat, she needs a new one. You're back in the shops comparing features and prices and will go home about one hundred pounds poorer. A travel seat is much more of a permanent feature in your car, as you tend not to carry it in or out every time you're going on a car journey. They look at lot like a Formula One driver's seat and you wouldn't mind sitting in one yourself, if they ever made them big enough.

**Pros:** Now that Baby is a few years old, she is taking a real interest in what's going on around her and spends less time asleep in the car. The car seat you need to be buying will provide support, comfort and enough height for the little one to look out of the window but will also have a reclining position for longer journeys. In fairness, you will get a lot more use out of a car seat than you did with the carry seat, so spending the extra pennies is more than justified.

**Cons:** The only real con to booster seats is that awkward year or so when your offspring is turning from infant to child. Once the head support is gone, your daughter will still fall asleep in the car but without anything to prop her up she'll tend to flop over to one side with only the seat-belt to stop her slumping into a little heap.

**What's it all about?** Go for a car seat which has a removable back, so that once your child is ready, you don't have to go out and buy a separate booster seat. If there are any occasions when other people are in the back of the car, be sure to check that the car seat is still securely fastened to the seat – older relations in particular have this uncanny ability to unbuckle the securing seatbelt thinking it is their own, leaving your child in an incredibly dangerous situation should you have an accident.

**Bloke's Rating:** This may be your only opportunity to buy zebra-skin patterned upholstery; grasp your chance while you can.

## Infant Head Support

**Description:** A very straightforward design that provides added head support for your baby or infant. Ideally suited for use in a car seat or in a pram, it's usually a length of foam or soft material contained within a fabric base that sits neatly around the head of your child to protect against sudden bumps, bangs and accidents and to keep Baby's wobbly head facing forward.

**Pros:** As a proportion of total body weight, the head is very heavy. Unfortunately for babies their neck muscles are almost non-existent and therefore Mum or Dad needs to help support the head of a baby for many weeks with one of these things. Adding a head support to the car seat also helps keep them warm.

**Cons:** You want to take your daughter to the shops to buy a couple of litres of milk and yet, by the time you have got her coat on, got her in the pushchair, got her strapped in and adjusted the head support, you've used up twenty minutes and it's almost time to come home again. But that's having young children for you. If you have a summer baby, then the only downside to head supports is that they can be a bit too warm during the hot weather.

**What's it all about?** You'll want to make Baby's world as comfortable as you can, especially in the early weeks because new babies sleep so much. By using an infant head support you'll be able to admire your snoozing child without constantly trying to reposition his head.

**Bloke's Rating:** Support is good.

## Car Shades

**Description:** Branded or plain, these simple mesh devices allow you to sort-of see through the rear windows while keeping the glare of the sun out.

**Pros:** The most obvious advantage to installing car shades is that your baby's retina are protected, but don't forget the subtler advantages, like when Baby is peacefully asleep in his seat and suddenly the brilliance of the sun bursts through the cloud cover, sending a beam of light right onto Baby's head. Without a car shade he's going to wake up and be grizzly.

**Cons:** I have found the branded car shades to be quite difficult to see through. You don't notice it much, but when you're trying to change lanes on the motorway or reverse-park and Baby's seat is behind the passenger, you'll be relying on instinct and blind luck. Put the child on the other side, you say, and that's all very well except when number two comes along.

**What's it all about?** Young babies aren't as adept at moving their eyes away from direct sunlight as you and me, and if they're strapped in tight to a car seat they haven't really got much option. Do them a favour and install at least one car shade.

**Bloke's Rating:** You may have made the decision outright never to put a 'baby on board' sticker in your car, but there's no getting away from the fact that once you put a car shade in, you now have a family car, not a babe magnet, no matter how flash your motor. Sorry.

## Baby Sling

**Description:** The beginner's baby carrier – an adjustable length of fabric which is draped around the shoulder to form a cradle or sling for an infant or toddler. Very similar, in fact, to a sling for a broken arm, only much bigger. The material is usually held in shape with a metal ring or clasp and your baby can be 'worn' on your front or on your back. It's what people used in olden times and continue to use today, especially in Asia and the Pacific Rim. Why? Because it works and it's a lot less bother and a lot cheaper than a baby carrier.

**Pros:** Cheap and cheerful, the sling offers the wearer some assistance with the weight of the baby or toddler, whilst still offering all of the benefits of a baby carrier – the proximity to Mum or Dad, the shared body warmth and the whole being carried *thang*. There's another advantage. Contrary to common sense there are certain members of the Great British public who actually think that mums shouldn't breast-feed in public. Why? They think it is a private affair that should be conducted behind closed doors. I still haven't worked out whether it is the sight of a baby receiving nourishment or a view of a bare breast that offends them, but complain they do and there have even been incidents of women being asked to put their waps away by the police because some Fascist OAP can't stand the fluctuations in his aorta because of an exposed lactating mammary gland. The knock-on effect of all this negative publicity and perceived animosity towards breastfeeding is that some mums do feel more comfortable disguising feeding time and the baby sling offers a practical solution by doubling as a privacy screen.

**Cons:** Some people think slings look a bit naff – the ethnic patterns and colours are often associated with new-age hippies and sweaty backpackers and therefore feel unsuitable for fashionable urban streets. It is possible to get hold of plain coloured slings, but it's quite hard.

**What's it all about?** The sling is a simple solution without the bells and whistles we find with so many baby gadgets. Are they naff? Well, that's down to personal taste. I can't pretend that many blokes would want to wear one, so the decision should really be left to your partner. If she wants to use it, go for it.

**Bloke's Rating:** Economic and traditional, which translates as – maybe not the best blokey status symbol.

## Baby Carriers (Front Load)

**Description:** A reverse backpack into which you place your baby, allowing you to carry her around while leaving your hands free to carry the nappy bag, camera, mobile phone and car keys. The alternative, of course, is to put all the baby stuff in a bag over your shoulder and carry your baby in your arms, but your arms will begin to ache very quickly.

**Pros:** Babies, despite their compact size, are remarkably heavy. Anyone who's enjoyed a sleepless night or two with a little one will vouch for me here. Newborns and young babies love to be close to another body, and while breast-feeding gives your partner a lot of body contact, there isn't much option for Dad – unless, of course, you get one of these little contraptions. Having your baby strapped to your chest is obviously great for her. She can enjoy your warmth, feel your chest move and generally feel very snug, and it's great for Dad to look down on her little head. Using the carrier will also mean you don't have to worry about carting a pram or a pushchair around, which can make nipping around the shops infinitely easier, especially on a Saturday. I favoured the carrier over the pushchair on particularly cold days so that our son could get the benefit of my jacket as well as his own.

**Cons:** Some dads have a bit of an issue wearing a baby carrier but once you've tried it on you will be converted. I would advise practising with the carrier on flat paths and roads before tackling any hills or walks over broken ground – there is something quite frightening about not being able to see your own feet, or the ground beneath you, and coupled with the responsibility of carrying your sleeping baby, that can make a simple stroll in the park a nerve-wracking experience. Your centre of balance will shift with the added weight on your chest, so slow, short steps are the key until you get used to the quite alien experience – it's totally different to being able to walk with a pack on your back. One disheartening fact is the oversight by manufacturers to include enough extendable strap to cater for a large-chested Dad and a larger baby – there might be a time when you simply can't adjust the thing any more and you'll have to revert to plan B – Mum gets to carry. Shame.

**What's it all about?** Some mums would argue that letting Dad carry the baby in a carrier is payback time for all the months your partner was carrying her in her womb. Maybe they're right, but it's hardly difficult. Enjoy it. And always remember when it comes to getting baby out, it's far easier than having to give birth – so, I guess we win again.

**Bloke's Rating:** Never mind how you look, it's how you feel that's important.

## Papooses and Baby Back Packs

**Description:** Harking back to the halcyon days of your Duke of Edinburgh's Award expedition, or your early boyhood dreams of soldiering, it's time to load up and move on out. Permission to wear a funky backpack in public and get away with it! A papoose is nothing more than a rucksack with two holes in the bottom for your baby's legs to stick out of. There are various options in terms of rain covers and extra pockets, but they all boil down to a rigid, or semi-rigid, frame and some material, be it canvas or plastic, to carry the baby.

**Pros:** As your baby gets ever bigger, you will need to transfer the weight from a front carrier to your back. Your spine and shoulders are able to cope with huge strains and now that Baby is able to keep his head up and wants to look around at the wildlife rather than snuffle into your chest, the papoose allows you to be incredibly mobile as a family. The distribution of weight across your back will allow for longer walks, striding through the great outdoors or toddling round the shops.

**Cons:** When you are first getting used to carrying your baby or toddler in a papoose, it can be worrying when they suddenly shift position. Have your partner or someone else walk behind you at first to confirm that baby is still well and truly strapped in and can't fall out, because that is exactly what it will feel like to you. As with some backpacks, prolonged use can result in Dad ending up with an unsightly sweat patch, which is fine while you're out walking and the papoose is on your back, but less so when you stop for a glass of orange and a scone at the village tea-shop. A small but quite annoying con can be the use of your head as a makeshift percussion instrument. Not so much of a concern when Baby is tapping out a rhythm with his hands, but can be quite painful if said rhythm is being counted out with a plastic cup, or a stick, or a stone.

**What's it all about?** The papoose, without doubt, has far more street cred than the front-load baby carrier. You really have no excuse. Whether you are a fan of long walks or not, it really is part and parcel of parenting and therefore you may as well make the exercise as pleasant as possible for yourself.

**Bloke's Rating:** Far, far, *far* less tiring and painful than having your toddler up on your shoulders.

## Hip Seat

**Description:** There comes the time when you need to pick up your offspring. Quite often, actually. That's fine; it's not so bad for the first five minutes or so, but then time begins to creep by, your partner has disappeared into the thick of the party or the frozen food aisle of the supermarket and you're left on the periphery... waiting, wondering, wishing... and carrying a very heavy baby. The hip seat is a funky accessory that comprises a thick belt and a padded seat onto which you sit your infant. You still have to hold on to them, but the strain is taken off your aching arm and shoulder.

**Pros:** This simple belt displaces the weight of your baby or toddler across the whole of your waist, which means you are able to hold him or her up for far longer. Baby is close by and comforted but you still have a free hand with which to stir dinner. Although it's your arm that first feels the burn of carrying a toddler, it is in fact your back that is really taking the strain and is likely to become injured from too much carrying. When we pick up babies and toddlers we tend to reposition ourselves awkwardly to compensate for the weight. As we favour our stronger arm, this bad positioning is repeated daily. Back pain is terrible and this little beauty can help you to avoid it.

**Cons:** Having a baby attached to you permanently can be bad enough, but when you start needing to wear a brace to lessen the impact and the strain, you know you're in trouble.

**What's it all about?** Take help wherever you can. Bringing up children is emotionally and physically draining, and a hip seat is the nearest you're going to get to an extra pair of helping hands. A hip seat will save on chiropractor fees.

**Bloke's Rating:** No matter how hard you think you are, that little baby is only going to get bigger. Swallow your pride and take a breather – wear the hipster and give your poor arms a break. All the other dads in the park won't laugh at you, I promise. Babies are heavy and you tried your best.

## Prams

**Description:** Both traditional-looking prams and the new hyper-modern variety are superb for carting the little one around from birth onwards. Most of the traditional prams will have a limited life span of about seven or eight months. The modern varieties will be good from birth right through to about three years.

**Pros:** Branding issues aside, the real benefit of prams is their capacity for storage – the amount of stuff you need to cart around in addition to your baby is phenomenal and the pram can help. A good one won't just be used when you are out and about – they're great for little daytime naps for very young babies, and for playtime, especially if you fit a colourful mobile or other, similar stimulant.

**Cons:** The limited life span of some prams really does not justify the cost, no matter how 'cute' or 'posh' the pram may look. Appearances, really, should be low down on your list of priorities. Prams can be incredibly bulky, which may prove an issue in terms of getting in and out of the house or shops. You also need to have the space to store the pram when Baby's not in it. Be realistic about the size of your home.

**What's it all about?** In an ideal world you want to be looking at getting a bulky pram which is suitable from birth right through to about six months and a lightweight buggy for your urban or travel needs. By having two options, you can decide which sort of transport works best for the chosen environment.

**Bloke's Rating:** Think urban-chic but also think about your wallet.

## Pushchairs

**Description:** Now that it is oh-so-funky to be a parent and especially to be a dad, the manufacturers have decided to go for it and capitalise on the change in attitudes. Pushchairs are now a sight to behold. With anything from three to eight wheels, they're at the forefront of design, innovation and sheer brilliant engineering. They appeal to mums as well as dads, but certainly the use of racing colours, strong lines and bizarre suspension systems seems to me at least to be a deliberate attempt to win Dad's custom.

**Pros:** Pushchairs are so much more comfortable for children than buggies. There's often a choice of reclining positions and the opportunity to attach all manner of toys, activities and essential accessories such as umbrellas and sunshades. Certainly the four- or eight-wheeled varieties are strong and stable and are more than adequate for all your country walks and long strolls. They are the Range Rover of the kids' mobility market, and, I suppose, are geared to appeal to a similar sort of buyer.

**Cons:** One major problem with some three-wheel pushchairs is their similarity to Robin Reliants – one sharp corner too many and they roll over. For most people that's not an issue, but the reality can be that they are somewhat unstable. We have a three-wheel pushchair and it has toppled over twice with our son on board: once when his over-zealous sister pulled on the side and once when he turned abruptly in his seat to watch a passing digger. The result on both occasions was a bloody lip – not much fun for him or for us. While pushchairs are fantastic for walks in the park, in a shop or on a narrow footpath they're like a Sherman tank.

**What's it all about?** Looks do come into it when we buy any product; to pretend that appearance is any less important when judging baby products is just false. Choose something that does look good, but also select a pushchair because it is comfortable, practical and sturdy.

**Bloke's Rating:** Go-faster stripes beat a Robin Reliant any day.

## Buggies

**Description:** Buggies come in a variety of shapes, sizes and colours. The varying price tags have little to do with the number of wheels and much more to do with their street cred and branding. Buggies are lightweight and effective, allowing you to nip around with your baby and providing you with an extra set of arms – the handlebars and any under-seat storage are great for all that shopping, and nappies, bottles, food, wipes, books and toys.

**Pros:** Buggies are particularly handy when you are travelling because they fold up and can be easily stowed on buses, aircraft and in cars. Buggies are nippy around town, especially in shops with narrow aisles and all of those other annoying shoppers who have deliberately chosen to come out shopping and stand in your way. Buggies can be basic, but most offer at least two positions – sitting and slightly reclined, which is great when you want your child to have a nap.

**Cons:** No matter how many years you have been shopping with a pushchair and child, every few weeks you will forget that there's fifty kilos of shopping hanging off the back. As you extract your child with minimum fuss, over the buggy will go with a thump and a crunch, and there will be broken eggs, tomatoes rolling everywhere and an abrupt end to that nice bottle of red you had planned to open that night. You're left trying to right the buggy with one arm and clutch the child in the other, while chasing those runaway tomatoes. When it happens in the privacy of your own hallway, it's bearable. When it happens in the middle of Boots on a Saturday afternoon it's a right pain in the arse.

**What's it all about?** Small, compact and incredibly useful, buggies are worth every penny. At the time of writing, Tesco were selling a basic buggy for less than twenty pounds. You can't argue with those prices.

**Bloke's Rating:** Have Buggy, Will Shop.

## Buggy Weights

**Description:** Small weights that can be fastened to the buggy above the front wheels. Why? Well, just by adding an additional two pounds of weight to one end, you can hang nearly twenty pounds on the back of the buggy – and who said physics was a waste of time?

**Pros:** Essential to avoid the buggy-tipping scenario. Most buggy weights come with a piece of reflective material, so there's an added 'be seen' safety element. Adding the weights will not stop you being able to fold the chair up when you need to store it or put it in the boot of the car. You are going to feel attached to your child's pushchair over the coming years; you may as well make it as convenient as you can.

**Cons:** None.

**What's it all about?** A simple solution for a common problem.

**Bloke's Rating:** Make your buggy the packhorse instead of yourself.

## Travel System

**Description:** Travel systems are a combination of all the above. You are buying a one-stop-solution to Baby's travel needs. Each travel system varies but basically you get a car seat and a pushchair/pram in one.

**Pros:** Getting Baby off to sleep can sometimes be really difficult. The last thing you want to do is wake her, but you might still need to leave the house again. The beauty of the travel system is that you can transfer the car seat out of the car, slot it onto the pushchair component and go off for a walk, without having to disturb Baby once. Travel systems really are geared up for parents who want a solution from birth onwards. One of the downsides of prams is that they are only really suitable from about six months onwards, and if you're going to want to cart Baby round a lot before then, the travel system is a great alternative to the traditional pram – and looks pretty cool too.

**Cons:** There's usually a high price tag associated with travel systems that can mean they are out of reach. However, if over the course of the next two years you are planning to buy a car seat, a pram and a pushchair, then the price is comparable.

**What's it all about?** The Audi TT of baby vehicles.

**Bloke's Rating:** Slick and sophisticated, just like you...

## Pram Extreme-Elements Bag (Cosy-Toes)

**Description:** You've been pushing your baby along in the pushchair and your fingers have gone numb. You're working your muscles and yet you are absolutely freezing and probably wondering why exactly you are out and about in such extreme weather. Well, Baby is thinking exactly the same thoughts – the only difference is that he isn't working any muscles and is sitting strapped into a pushchair against his will. He's cold, bored and as far as he is concerned, this is never-ending. There was a reason you came out, even if that reason was just to stretch your legs, but that's irrelevant to your baby; he wants to be warm right here and right now. What can you do about it? You can buy a Cosy-Toes bag right away and keep Baby toasty and warm. A Cosy-Toes bag is basically a sleeping bag that attaches to your pushchair to offer some serious warmth during the coldest of winters. Baby is strapped in and then zipped up, leaving only his face exposed and you can do all your winter wandering without endangering your child.

**Pros:** It's quite hard for babies to fall asleep in the pushchair during the winter months, especially if there's a gale-force wind blowing into their face and their fingers have turned purple with cold. With a Cosy-Toes bag Baby should be able to sleep in his chair no problem.

**Cons:** All that extra padding does get in the way of the straps, and you might find that the Cosy-Toes bag moves around when your child's wriggling about, so in all it's a whole lot harder to get him strapped in.

**What's it all about?** Comfort and warmth for your child during the bleakest of British winters.

**Bloke's Rating:** It's only fair.

## Ride-on Toys – Indoors

**Description:** Whether you choose a wild animal or a vehicle or even a children's TV character design, ride-on toys are a fantastic way to give your toddler confidence in taking his first steps and will provide hours of entertainment once they are able to ride unassisted. The design you choose will no doubt be based on something your toddler really likes, or else it will have been bought and given by a friend or family member as a present. Either way, you are now on-track to giving your toddler a taste of independence. Whatever the cost, bear in mind that eventually they'll be asking for a set of wheels themselves and then you'll be looking at buying a car – or having to let them use yours – along with insurance, car tax and a whole heap of lessons.

**Pros:** Assuming you are not too precious about your freshly painted skirting boards, ride-on toys are great fun. Initially kids like to push them around. For a few weeks there will be the painful process of watching Baby trying to cock a leg and mount the toy, which invariably results in him toppling over in a mess of limbs, but perseverance is the key and before you know it, Junior is negotiating corners, obstacles and insisting he should ride through the magic tunnel – your straddled legs – for months, and months, and months. They love it. You might have another opinion.

**Cons:** The early days of ride-on toys will result in a number of spectacular headfirst dives over the steering wheel or handlebars. After a few weeks this will be replaced with the occasional mere sideways fall resulting in nothing more than a scrape or a bruise. After a few months – assuming you don't allow your child to try riding down the staircase – you are home and dry. Getting to grips with steering is something we have all struggled with – my wife would say I still haven't quite managed it, given the number of passenger door mirrors we've had to replace over the years – and your toddler will roar with frustration when the ride-on toy won't do precisely what they want.

**What's it all about?** The appearance of ride-on toys in the house spells the end of a truly tidy house. No longer can all evidence of little ones be hidden away in boxes and cupboards of an evening. Although you can park the vehicle or vehicles in a corner of the room, there's no getting away from the fact that your toddler is making his mark on the landscape of your home. Next stop, the art gallery on the kitchen wall – that's if it's not there already.

**Bloke's Rating:** Ride on!

## Ride-on Toys – Outdoors

**Description:** Often just big chunky hunks of plastic, these simple cars, trikes and trucks are probably the greatest value for money in terms of hours of pleasure for your pound.

**Pros:** For minimum outlay you get a toy that seems to transcend the age ranges, unlike practically every other product you will buy for your kids. For once there truly is lasting appeal, a real sense that your money could not have been better spent elsewhere. Ride-on toys are fun for your kids and as they become more confident you can start to introduce simple ramps and obstacles for them to manoeuvre over. Children start to learn to play alone, especially with the wheeled variety, and obviously they have a beneficial effect on hand/eye co-ordination.

**Cons:** If you have a small, beautiful garden, then the last thing you want is to see it cluttered with garish plastic toys – but you'll have to put your sensibilities on hold, because it's your baby's garden as much as it is yours, and that means sharing. No, come on. Share. That's right. Good boy.

Gone are the up-and-down lines of a freshly mown lawn and in come the skid marks, craters and general disaster-area of a garden given over to children's play. Bet you wish you'd just concreted the whole thing.

**What's it all about?** Both of our children can't get enough of their plastic truck; it has no pedals and needs to be pushed along by leg power. Every child that comes round to the house rides on it, it's been thrown around, abused, kicked, left out in the rain, thrown off the balcony and yet it continues to give pleasure. This thing is indestructible and must have cost about fourteen pounds about five years ago.

**Bloke's Rating:** Time outside is obviously important, but young children don't want to appreciate your hydrangeas – they want excitement and fun. Give the little tykes something from Little Tykes.

## Ride-on Toys – with Sticks for Parents to Push

**Description:** All your favourite animals, cartoon characters and emergency service vehicles are represented; the only difference is that, this time, you the parent are expected to get involved. That's right, not only are there pedals or a hole in the floor for the little one to motor around, but there's also a dirty big stick with a nice comfy hand grip that's just calling out to be grabbed and pushed. That's right, Dad – that's your job, that is. Sucker!

**Pros:** None whatsoever.

**Cons:** Buying one of these is a complete con. Don't do it. Please.

**What's it all about?** You are so setting yourself up for a fall with one of these little devices. All you're doing is giving the child the excuse to be lazy. Not like they need much of an excuse. There's no escaping the fact that you will have to push. In fact, you'll have to push constantly – up hills, in shops, down escalators, through fields, in zoos and across busy roads. Don't do it. And don't let doting grandparents sneak one into the house at birthdays or Christmas either.

**Bloke's Rating:** Don't! It could kill you.

## Wheely Bugs

**Description:** These are without doubt the last word in ride-on technology. Simple design, stunning appearance and it'll keep your toddler amused for hours. Our five-year-old still plays with hers, three years on. The Wheely Bugs come in a number of designs, including a bee, a ladybird, a mouse and a cow. They are available in two sizes – small (6 months–2 years) and large (12 months–3 years).

**Pros:** The reason I feel the Wheely Bug is such an important toy is its 360-degree capability. A huge fault with many of the push-along/ride-on toys is their insistence on regular wheels, either fixed with bolts or connected to an axle, limiting the child's directional options and requiring a considerable amount of practice and a fundamental under-standing of physics to master. Quite a lot to ask from a child under two, don't you think? Throw in the concept of a steering wheel and the toy may prove to be more frus-trating than fun. With the Wheely Bug castors, your child can decide to change direction without thought. The Bug will comply and the net result is that there are fewer nasty falls and tantrums.

**Cons:** The only problem we've experienced is one of the castors falling off after some serious usage. Easily remedied with a spanner.

**What's it all about?** The Wheely Bug works best on smooth surfaces – tiles, lino, laminate floors. If you're a deep shag sort of a household you might find they stick a bit on carpet. As well as their being available from specialist toyshops, you can find Wheely Bugs reasonably priced on eBay.

**Bloke's Rating:** Top banana. I can't recommend them enough. Sheer brilliance.

## Rocking Toys

**Description:** Cheap as chips and yet they offer so much. Why? Because kids love them, and once they're able to get on and off unaided there's no stopping them. That leaves you a welcome ten minutes to watch their endless pleasure while glancing over the supplements in the Sunday newspaper – and it's been a long time since you were able to do that. Rocking toys are big and bold and come in a huge variety of animal shapes.

**Pros:** If nothing else, rest assured that rocking toys improve the leg muscles and the balance of the baby or child involved. Keep up the encouragement and don't lose sight of the goal – next stop, riding a bike.

**Cons:** The early days of rockers come with a fair share of toppling over and a preference for pushing the thing around rather than sitting and, well, rocking, but everything's a learning curve. Over-confident kids start to rock quite alarmingly when they get a bit older, but I haven't seen one actually go airborne yet.

**What's it all about?** Virtually indestructible, this could be the best ten pounds you ever spend on your child.

**Bloke's Rating:** A must for every garden and back yard.

## Bike Trailer

**Description:** You don't just trade in the racing green MG-F for a beige Volvo estate when you become a dad. Oh, no. Even your new mountain bike is no longer safe from the ever-pervasive effect of having children. Just as you'd got your 10km sprint down to an admirable time, you arrive home to find that you've got a bike trailer. What can you do? Well, the simple answer is to attach the trailer to the rear of your bike and get pedalling while your toddler rides along in state like Lady Muck.

**Pros:** It's singing the praises of the great outdoors again, but this time with a real healthy lifestyle option thrown in for you too. The bike trailer actually allows some dads more of an opportunity to ride their bike than they had before. If you are someone who promises themselves on the Monday that you will go for a quick ride on the Saturday, then chances are by the time the weekend comes you'll be too knackered or preoccupied with the Grand Prix qualifiers to get round to it. If, however, you or your partner has mentioned to your toddler that you are going for a ride on Saturday, and that they're going too, well, then there's absolutely no way of getting out of it. And don't think a bit of British rain is going to give you a last-minute reprise. No way, pal. The trailers are fully covered and waterproof.

You're going for that cycle ride, my friend, and you're the only one who's going to get wet!

Jokes aside, it is marvellous to include the little one in as many activities as you can. You get fit and they have fun. That's killing two birds with one stone, that is. There are some particularly groovy models that come with a detachable third wheel and a handle, which means the bike trailer doubles as a pushchair – perfect if you are in training for a biathlon.

**Cons:** Prices for trailers will vary depending on the manufacturer and it can all get quite pricey. However, if cycling is something you do often, or want to start doing often, then things like bike helmets will be a necessity along with the fluorescent jackets, pump, waterproofs and the all-important triangular orange flag.

**What's it all about?** Kids love travelling on a bike trailer and you will love it too. If you are concerned about how busy the roads are nowadays, then pack the whole lot up in the car and drive to a park or a coastal promenade. It's easy to snigger at bike trailers, but you're just making excuses. Get out there and give it a go and then decide.

**Bloke's Rating:** Good clean fun.


## Trailer Bikes/Wheels

**Description:** Basically it's like sticking half an extra bike onto the back of your own. What you are creating is a tandem bike, but I must say it looks a little bit cooler and, when Junior's not about, you can easily disengage it from your own bike and pretend the whole thing never happened.

The Trailer Bike works in a similar way to the canvas Bike Trailer, in that it pivots when you take corners, but will encourage far more interaction from your child in that it offers the chance to pedal and hold on to handlebars as well.

**Pros:** Trailer Bikes are a fantastic confidence booster for children in preparation for when they will eventually go it alone, which is not something I am particularly looking forward to, but, like the inevitable time when my daughter brings home her first boyfriend – or girlfriend? – it's a day that will eventually creep up on me and take me by complete surprise.

By installing a trailer bike you are encouraging outdoor activities but if you're really cruel, you can stop pedalling completely and let your offspring power you around the park – but you can definitely expect complaints.

**Cons:** The only real con, in my opinion, is the cost. Expect to pay about one hundred pounds for what is essentially a glorified unicycle. It seems a bit steep. However, once you've bought one you know it will last a long time, and, at that price you're likely to make sure that it is used.

**What's it all about?** Trailer Bikes are a fantastic way to get kids comfortable with bicycles. For parents who use a Trailer Bike, the responsibility of the school run can be shared with your child, especially if you are both responsible for peddling. What better way to get to school and back every day than sharing a bike ride, come rain or shine. It's so easy to be scathing and critical – but as naff as it looks, it's pretty cool to have your offspring riding pillion with you down those mean streets.

**Bloke's Rating:** If the roads aren't too busy and your child is up for it, why not?

## Bike Seat

**Description:** Er – a seat that you attach to your bike for a baby or younger toddler to sit in. Not a lot to it, really. Most are secured to the saddle of your bike and the bike seat sits neatly over the rear wheel, but you can also get smaller seats that fix to the front of the bike.

**Pros:** It can be more reassuring for you if your baby is up high behind Dad, rather than trailing behind in a canvas sack on wheels. Having your child so close means that you can keep up a running commentary or conversation with the little one, assuming you aren't panting for breath and close to collapsing with fatigue, and you have some welcome company as you pedal about. Bike seats are a great way to get your very young child comfortable with the whole concept of cycling, which is handy for when they eventually get their own two wheels.

**Cons:** Having a baby fixed to a seat which in turn is fixed to your bike can be a little scary, especially if you haven't ridden a bike in a number of years. As most children aren't actually concentrating on balancing, their sudden movements can and will influence your own equilibrium and I would recommend a lot of practice in the park before ever venturing on to the open road with an occupied bike seat. A bike seat will add extra drag to your performance, but by the time you have attached one you will in any case have given up any aspirations to win or even compete in *Le Tour*.

**What's it all about?** As with most aspects of parenting, it requires maximum effort from you for a negligible return for your child – and based on that logic, it's a must. Baby seat users think we're all missing out terribly.

**Bloke's Rating:** Personally, I don't trust my own cycling ability enough to ever dream of attaching a baby seat to my bike – never mind filling the seat with my own flesh and blood.

## Pram Rider/Board

**Description:** A pram board is a plastic plate that attaches to the back of a pushchair, allowing you to cart a tired child around as you push your smaller infant now that the new baby has stolen the older child's carriage. A pram *rider* is a far more exotic mobile seat on wheels, not dissimilar to a motorbike sidecar that again attaches to the pushchair but allows your older child to sit rather than stand – put a pair of goggles on him and you can recreate scenes from *The Great Escape* again and again and again.

**Pros:** Although as parents we want to encourage our kids to walk under their own steam, sometimes their snail's pace is painfully slow. The more adventurous amongst you may well get carried away with a Sunday stroll and find your older child can't cope with the miles you are clocking up and just decides enough is enough and sits themselves down on the pavement, refusing to budge. It is during these moments that the canny parent who has remembered to attach a pram rider can now offer their oh-so-tired child the opportunity to be pushed along in comfort.

**Cons:** Given the opportunity to walk or ride, most kids are going to take the easy choice. The pram board takes a bit of effort to attach and detach, so you can't really take it off at the start of the outing and make the older child do at least a bit of walking before he rides home. Expect a tantrum or two if you want to insist he stretches his legs first.

**What's it all about?** When there is a gap of over two years between children it seems a bit pointless buying a double buggy, because the oldest is quite capable of walking. However, for many of us with a gap between kids that is roughly two years or less, this is an absolute necessity. A pram rider or board can be a complete life-saver.

**Bloke's Rating:** You can live without it but if you ever want to be on time for anything again, you need one.

# Training

We all want our children to be fighting fit and ready for the many challenges they will have to face throughout life. Those first trials happen early – from day one, really. The speed with which your baby starts to crawl, stand up and walk marks a new milestone every time. They are also highly competitive rites of passage. Try as you might not to get involved, you will invariably be sucked in – comparisons will be made between the apple of your eye and every other baby that you know. To make matters worse, other people will make comparisons with babies you do not know, or even worse, with babies that aren't even babies any more.

'Yes, son, but you were walking when you were seven days old and Uncle Frank was working in the factory before his second birthday.'

How clouded our memory becomes. The truth of the

matter is that every baby is unique and will get round to doing things in their own sweet time. No amount of pressure from you is really going to bring forward his first steps or a full set of pearly-white teeth – but that doesn't stop us from trying. We wouldn't feel like effective parents if we weren't at least encouraging development in our children. We naturally want them to succeed. We want them to be the best, the tallest, the fastest, the strongest. Thankfully – or conveniently – a number of manufacturers have bent over backwards to ensure that there is a massive selection of products available to ensure you can help train your baby to do absolutely anything. But buy with caution.

As with all baby gadgets, some educational products are useful and some not so useful. The main problem with the apparatus designed to help your child 'develop' is that babies are all very different. Just because little Emily down the road spends four hours a day in her bouncer and loves it, does not necessarily mean that your baby will. Some kids like red toys and some like blue. Every time you consider buying your child an educational gadget, be prepared for the chance that it will be used once for thirty seconds and then ignored until you eventually pass it on to another child or take it to the charity shop.

On the flip side, your baby's world should be one of adventure and discovery. Her mind needs stimulation and something different to find, and find again and again, round about every fifteen minutes. Be sure yours is a house of variety, not a barren wasteland of Mum-and-Dad stuff with which Baby is not allowed to play.

## Baby Gyms

**Description:** A soft, comfortable surface over which hang two arcing poles and under which events may dazzle and amaze the onlooker – not dissimilar, in fact, to the new Wembley Stadium. Or more precisely, a selection of toys and soft cuddly things suspended from above that will entertain your baby as she tries to focus on this strange planet she's just arrived in.

**Pros:** Baby gyms show you, the parent, the wide array of feats and movements that your baby can manage even though she's only a few months old. Once you put Junior under those activity toys you'll begin to see a total-body experience taking place, with all sorts of leg and foot action going on as well as the first real utilisation of fists and arms – it's truly remarkable. Baby gyms, for most of us, are the first opportunity we get to see Baby flexing her muscles and choosing which toys she likes and which toys she doesn't.

**Cons:** It's not really the fault of the baby gym, but there is something quite sad about the time when baby has had enough of being static on the floor and just wants to explore instead. As parents we obviously applaud the newfound skills of crawling and, very soon, walking, but equally we mourn the end of the true baby-era. Baby takes a matter of months to go from cute, near-helpless infant lying prone on the floor to the destroyer that is a toddler, roaming from room to room upsetting all that stands in his or her path. Never mind 'Pity the children'; how about 'Pity my brand-new state-of-the-art LCD stuck-to-the-wall television'?

**What's it all about?** Babies either get on with gyms or they don't. There's no real way of telling until you have gone to the trouble of buying one. Our son would certainly use his, but only if one of us was hovering over him and encouraging every single interaction – whereas friends of ours unveiled their baby gym one day and by the next, their baby was lost in her own world for the best part of two hours at a time. This gave Mum and Dad the chance to read a chapter of their new paperback, or watch a bit of news on the television. Imagine that.

**Bloke's Rating:** You've joined the gym yourself in the past, and had every intention of going regularly – this could be the same for your little one. Give them a while to get into it. Alternate the toys, and therefore the exercises on offer, and look forward to the day that he rolls over for the first time, unassisted – magic.

## Door Bouncers

**Description:** Always fancied a go at parachuting? Well, this won't help, but for a brief second when you first see your baby strapped into one of these contraptions you can wonder what it might be like to jump head-first from a Hercules at 15,000 feet and imagine that all that's getting in the way of certain death are some lengths of material sewn or fused together by an underpaid machinist in Burnley. Still want to sign up for that red-letter day?

Door bouncers are fantastic. So simple, yet, if your baby likes them, they can be the source of many minutes and hours of entertainment. Once you have attached the rather powerful spring lock to the doorframe, insert your baby and let them get on with it. The spring-assisted straps allow baby to taste the wonders of bipedal existence a few months before their little leg muscles are able to take the strain. The gentlest of movements sends them bouncing up and down – and sometimes from left to right – and into fits of giggles and broad smiles.

**Pros:** There's no real proof that a bouncer will lead to your baby standing and walking any faster than if you don't use one, but there's no denying that encouraging the use of the leg muscles must be helping to strengthen and prepare her for her first steps. Once we introduced a door bouncer at about five months, we found our daughter was less clingy thanks to her experience of 'assisted independence'. She would bounce for about twenty minutes a day.

**Cons:** Do leave it for a while after milk or meals otherwise you run the risk of Baby being sick. Be sure to only use a bouncer when the door frame sticks out proud from the wall above, otherwise there's a risk that the downward motion could pull the spring from the door, which wouldn't be much fun at all. Door bouncers don't work for every child. Our daughter loved using it, our son preferred to do anything but.

**What's it all about?** Bouncers are a bit like a mini-bungee experience for kids. They store away after use and as long as you don't start trying to catapult your son or daughter across the room, they're completely safe.

**Bloke's Rating:** Let them earn their wings.


## Push- or Pull-along toys

**Description:** Whether it is a caterpillar, dog or random unidentified animal on a string, it really doesn't matter. Sometimes babies bond to their pull-along toys as if there might actually be a maternal or paternal bond. Don't worry: this is obviously a load of rubbish. They really do love you, but sometimes a bright red dog or a yellow caterpillar just has more appeal to your little one. Sorry, Dad. Babies love push-/pull-along toys – it is a simple undisputable fact. You can't really complain too much about jealousy. It was probably you who bought the thing in the first place!

**Pros:** The first toys that our children choose to play with, in a way, begin to define them as human beings. Our daughter took a particular fancy to a blanket which was given to her as one of many first-birthday presents. Our son was given a small blue bunny rabbit – a toy, not the real thing – and that has been his favourite since the day he first learnt to grab. These are the items that our children simply can't live without, but the veritable army of push-/pull-along toys that has massed under the stairs and in every single cupboard in our house comes a close second. There are simple wooden pull-alongs, like the classic nodding spotty dog, and then there are the complex, noisy, plastic musical pull-alongs that offend the local cat population and for some strange reason never seem to run out of batteries.

**Cons:** Having children adds a decibel or two to the general ambience of a home. Part of the increased noise will be the emissions from your son and heir, but push-/pull-along toys make their own significant contribution. The simple wooden pull-along toys that clatter away to themselves are fine, but the plastic electronic versions are a complete pain in the arse. Not only will they annoy you throughout the day, but just as you've got the little one off to sleep in the evening and you're tidying up the mess, you'll trip over one of the little buggers. It only takes one small flick, movement or a blatant kick and you'll end up with a high-volume Casio concerto on seemingly endless repeat. There's nothing worse than waking your baby up to the sound of his favourite toy. If you've ever wondered why people throw things into canals – here's the answer.

**What's it all about?** Hours of fun for your precious babes, but choose your toy wisely, or you're chucking money down the drain – or in the canal, to be more precise.

**Bloke's Rating:** You can't escape push-/pull-along toys, so don't even try. There is definitely a photo opportunity to be had with the little one dragging a large green plastic caterpillar along the floor – but wise is the dad who refuses to put batteries in right from the start. What they don't know won't hurt them.

## Shape-Sorters

**Description:** Plastic or wood, it really doesn't make much of a difference. This is basic problem-solving and a game that you can be very much involved in. The task at hand is to squeeze the correct coloured shape through the corresponding hole. Not dissimilar to your or my own attempts to make babies in the first place – simple, yet tricky, and it's a lot of fun trying.

Get it right and the piece of wood or plastic falls into the box underneath, get it wrong and it feels like banging your head against a wall. Despite the fact that all young children are easily frustrated, for some bizarre reason they will persist with a shape-sorter until they get it right. Observing a toddler on a mission to succeed is a sight in itself – the bloody-minded determination is a lesson to us all. Why it stops with the shape-sorter and doesn't continue when it comes to eating vegetables is a complete mystery, but there you go.

**Pros:** To watch your own child struggle with the effort of trying to squeeze a large circular block through a small square hole is a lesson in self-control. Yes, you want Baby to understand the concept and succeed at the task; yes, you will find it difficult not to rip the piece of plastic from your own son's hands in a bid to complete the puzzle, but once you leave your frustration behind it becomes a fascinating psychological experiment watching them fail again and again. Please remember that it may seem very straightforward to you that the yellow triangle shape fits into the yellow triangle hole – but you've had experience of such matters.

**Cons:** The first few weeks of using a shape-sorter can be very trying. Baby is determined to squeeze the rhombus shape into the oval hole and it just isn't happening. Net result: the tears start flowing and your small child starts hitting you and then throws small pieces of plastic across the room. Hey, this is supposed to be fun, you say to yourself, over and over like a mantra. And it is. Persevere. Give it a few weeks and suddenly you'll realise that you have a little Einstein on your hands. All of those shapes and all of those options and suddenly the blue shape fits in the blue hole and the small circle fits in the large square hole – and everything is complete.

How sweet the moment when your toddler suddenly *gets it* and begins to systematically place the correct piece in the correct hole – all at once you appreciate your child on a completely different level. You're not just giving marks out of ten for cuteness; you're beginning to see their cognitive abilities and I don't think there's anything that'll give you a warmer, fuzzier glow.

**What's it all about?** Reasoning and problem-solving both begin at the toddler stage of development. A child who does not have the joy and challenge of a shape-sorter hasn't lived. We all meet challenges on a daily basis which can prove frustrating and irrational. Although we all want the best for our kids, we also have to prepare them for the real world – even if they are a mere eighteen months old. Let them experiment with the shape-sorter. Only through failure will they succeed.

**Bloke's Rating:** Do your child a favour: buy a shape-sorter, encourage them, share their frustration of getting it wrong and, equally, share their joy of getting it right. Bear in mind that if they can manage a shape-sorter, then the next stop is managing director of a large plc. You think I'm joking? Well, just wait and see.

## Swing

**Description:** A swing is big and bulky, but how much kudos does it add to a garden? Lots. Especially when you are planning to sell to newly-weds who either are already or soon will be planning to have children. Swings can also make the most boring and barren back yard look appealing and fun.

**Pros:** Introducing a swing to the garden may mean an accident or two over the coming few years, but you'll still go ahead and buy one anyway. Most kids love swings – I say most because my son hates going anywhere near them. I might as well be offering him the chance to walk on broken glass, given the expression of disgust and horror he pulls when I even mention the word. Maybe it's just Ronin and every other child in the world loves swings – who knows? As well as regular swings which involve a simple length of plastic or wood for a child to sit on, you can of course buy baby swings, which have a cage around the seating area especially suitable for younger children who simply do not under-stand what it means to hold on, no matter how many times you might remind them.

There's an additional benefit to swings, for Mummy and Daddy; I mean, you own it and it's in your garden and if your partner wants to sit on it naked and you just happen to be standing opposite her, without any shorts and it's dark and you... can make up the rest, it's pretty obvious... That's a bonus, isn't it?

**Cons:** Occasional accidents. It's not a dead cert but no matter how much time you spend on hand to monitor proceedings, there's always a chance that a momentary lapse in concentration will result in a bloodied knee and a bruised ego. When you've picked yourself up from the floor and brushed yourself down, you should wipe away your tears and let your child have a go on the swing and pretend the whole nasty incident never took place. Of course, it also means the absolute and total destruction of the patch of grass directly below the swing – all that foot-scuffing will leave a permanent scar on your lawn.

**What's it all about?** Learning to swing isn't as straight-forward as it may at first seem. My daughter, for example, has loved being on a swing from an early age but has only just accepted that she no longer needs Daddy to keep pushing her. She's now five. Buying a swing is a commitment – you may well be hearing the plea, 'Daddy, can you push me?' even during sub-zero temperatures, for many, *many* years to come.

**Bloke's Rating:** Swing when you're winning.

## Outdoor Play Sets

**Description:** Again there is a range of products available to suit every garden and every pocket, but what you want for your money is some kind of climbing apparatus, maybe a tunnel or two, a slide and sometimes a swing or a fire-fighter's pole. In a nutshell, your very own activity park – with the added benefit of not having to share the features with that horrible snotty-nosed six-year-old who terrorises your little boy at the public park. Outdoor play sets are generally made from chunky plastic sections that all fit together very easily. There are still metal and wooden sets available, but they tend to be at the top end of the price bracket.

**Pros:** If you have got the space, and the cash, your garden gives you another option during the day to stimulate your child and keep their activity levels up as long as the weather is amenable. It's a given that on the days when children play outside they seem to sleep and sometimes even eat better than when they are cooped up inside. Fresh air simply knackers them out – and that's a good thing when it comes to bedtime. We're not all fortunate enough to have a fantastic play park at the end of the road, and if there is a park at all it can sometimes be closed due to vandalism or other nefarious goings-on from the night before. Sometimes it can be a real effort to get to the local swings, especially if they're not that local, and having an outside play option in your own garden or yard is a blessing for both Dad and Baby.

**Cons:** There's investing in your child and then there's spoiling him rotten. You can spend hundreds or even thousands on an all-singing, all-dancing model. Just because you would have really liked to have had one when you were a little boy doesn't necessarily mean that you should throw caution to the wind and laugh in the face of rising credit-card debt.

Encouraging your child to climb – maybe before they are ready – can lead to nasty falls and your toddler getting scared, but equally we can't coddle them stupid. I remember playing for hours on climbing frames and I lived to tell the tale, so it can't be all that bad.

**What's it all about?** Let your child taste the great outdoors as much as possible. Unfortunately they're not old enough to appreciate the clean air and the birdsong quite yet, but they will enjoy climbing over something that's bright purple and made of plastic.

**Bloke's Rating:** Far better than watching telly.

## Paddling Pool

**Description:** Paddling pools can be straightforward inflatable containers to which you just add water, or they can be complex constructions featuring castles, slides and even trampoline attachments, but one thing is for sure, kids love them, and on a balmy summer's afternoon, the larger ones can even accommodate Dad.

**Pros:** Hours and hours and hours of fun.

**Cons:** There's an obvious danger with water, no matter how shallow it is, so paddling pools can only ever be a supervised activity, but when the sun's shining, what other excuse do you need to spend a few hours out in the garden? Buy an air pump – filling even the smallest of pools with lung-power alone will leave you dizzy and wallowing in self-pity at your failing, ageing cardio-vascular ability. Save yourself the shame.

Explaining a hosepipe ban to a three-year-old is never an easy argument to conduct. If you do find yourself caving in, finish off the day's paddling by adding some bubbles and giving your child a good scrub – that way you are only giving your child an outdoor bath, which no neighbour in their right mind is going to prevent you from doing. Tenuous, I know, but it has worked for us.

**What's it all about?** Getting kids used to water is only going to help when it comes to learning how to swim. Although Britain is an island, it's a big island and most of us don't live next to the sea, nor can we afford a million visits to the swimming baths. A paddling pool is chlorine- and wee-free – well, it may only contain their wee, which is different – and far cheaper than a holiday for three in Greece.

**Bloke's Rating:** Fun in the sun.

## Playpen

**Description:** A play area for babies, contained within mesh sides or bars. Usually playpens are a little larger than a cot, and some have handy gates to get Baby in and out. Playpens have nice soft floorings and once you've added a few of her favourite toys, it's an Aladdin's cave of fun for the little one.

**Pros:** Assuming that your child is happy to be penned in, then the playpen is a fantastic invention allowing the caring parent to get on with other things, like the washing-up that is still there from breakfast time. You can use the playpen to store lots of toys and when Baby is playing the tall sides keep most of the toys in. Babies who really like playpens can even fall asleep in mid-play and wake up again an hour later and keep on playing.

**Cons:** Most children aren't happy to be penned up in a confined area, especially once they start crawling. Playpens do seem like a great idea and our parents' promise us that we were more than happy to spend the first sixteen years of our life in one, but it simply isn't true, or at least it doesn't seem to appeal to today's kids as much as it appealed to our generation. The grass is always greener and babies can get very upset if they're dumped in the playpen when everyone else is allowed to wander around and do what they want.

**What's it all about?** Playpens work for some kids and not for others. Don't be too disappointed if it doesn't work out. Remember when choosing a playpen for your home that, even though they fold up, they're not small.

**Bloke's Rating:** Let your baby try out a playpen at someone else's house before you buy one of these contraptions.

## Baby Walker

**Description:** Although this toy is very traditional, they are in fact incredibly contemporary – maybe not in design, but certainly in the choice of materials used. It is still possible to get a baby walker with wooden blocks but most are large plastic A-frames with all manner of knobs, squeaky things, buttons and dials to entertain and amuse your child.

**Pros:** Walkers, whether they're made from plastic or wood, are great devices to encourage Baby to stand on his own two feet. They provide support for your child's first steps and give them the taste of independent walking while still being able to hold on to something. Long after Baby is walking unaided the walker is still lots of fun to push around.

**Cons:** If you go for the wooden block walker then be warned that your child will hide a block somewhere that is inaccessible to you or Mum and without fail you will be blamed for the loss of the brick because it went missing on your watch. Walkers are sturdy and therefore when they are aggressively introduced to skirting boards and wooden doors they tend to leave a mark, or a chip, or a dent. Or all three. If there are older children in the house, then, at some stage, the walker will be 'borrowed' and no doubt broken.

**What's it all about?** Simple but effective, these Zimmer-frames for kids are a firm favourite in every household. Especially useful on cold or wet days when you want to encourage exercise but can't leave the house.

**Bloke's Rating:** Walk on, walk on, with hope in your heart…

# Clothing and Kit Bags

Whether you are a fan of designer clothes or not, it's of paramount importance that you equip your child with the vast array of clothes necessary to exist in modern-day Britain. By that I mean she needs to be prepared for the best and the worst of weather systems. It's all very well buying a selection of T-shirts for every day of the week, but what happens during the winter of discontent, when temperatures drop, natural gas is too expensive and you are not allowed to burn anything in your fireplace? You go shopping is what you do.

Kitting out your offspring doesn't stop with clothes and apparel; oh, no. The list of gadgets and products you need, or are encouraged to buy, is endless and you'll need to start buying some of it right now. Some decisions you will be making in the near future will be very important

– especially the question of whether to use disposable or reusable nappies. Other decisions – like having a fancy-dress costume for every day of the week – are more down to what interests your child and how much you are willing to spend on them. Everything on offer does have a use, but it will be down to you as parents to decide whether you actually *need* them or not.

## Winter Body Suits

**Description:** In no other garment can a child look so cuddly and cute as well as utterly pathetic at the same time. His legs and arms don't seem to work properly, nor do they fill all of the available space. Baby appears to be wrapped in so many thermal layers, it's a complete surprise he doesn't start to boil.

**Pros:** The temperature of babies can change drastically in a matter of minutes. They are not very good at regulating themselves and the adding or removing of layers has an instant effect. When you want or need to brave the winter elements with a baby, you must ensure they are as toasty as possible, and that is exactly what a body suit will guarantee.

**Cons:** Other than you having to remember to unzip the body suit once you are safely inside the warmth of your home, or other destination, there isn't much to say against them. Do adjust the straps on the baby car seat and the pushchair in advance, to allow for the extra bulk of material. I suppose that the downside is that these things can be quite pricey and, given how fast babies grow, you really will only get one season's wear out of the thing – but that's pretty much true of all baby clothes and maybe it's just another great excuse to buy more next year.

**What's it all about?** On the piste or not, it's the only chance you'll get to dress him up in an all-in-one bright yellow snowsuit.

**Bloke's Rating:** A real photo opportunity – oh, and it will keep your son very warm.

## Hats

**Description:** You know, a hat. A bit of material that you put on your head to keep it warm or cool. Well, your baby's head, that is. From the sublime to the sophisticated, from the serious to the silly, there's a whole raft of hats for sale, specially designed for kids.

**Pros:** Er. Well, a winter hat will keep Baby warm and a summer hat will keep him feeling cool. Simple, really. In all seriousness, we lose 70% of all our body heat through our heads. That's absolutely incredible. If Baby goes hatless in the winter he's going to feel the cold very fast and it doesn't really make much difference how warm his coat is. Hats are generally quite cheap and there is no shame in building up a bit of a collection. There's a hat for every conceivable weather system.

**Cons:** Make sure any hat you buy has straps, a buckle, elastic, a ribbon, a jubilee clip or anything in fact that means the hat can somehow fasten under the chin – it's the only way the thing is going to stay on. Add at least another five minutes to the 'getting-out-of-the-house-takes-nearly-half-an-hour' routine.

**What's it all about?** Just because you prefer not to wear hats, or for that matter even wear a jacket when you're out and about does not mean that your daughter doesn't need those items of clothing either. Leave the box of hats, scarves and gloves at or near the door so that you have to physically walk past it to get out of the house.

**Bloke's Rating:** Essential, but expect to lose a few over the years.

## Gloves

**Description:** You don't need me to tell you what gloves are, but you do need to remember that you have two options – gloves with fingers, and mittens.

**Pros:** Gloves without separate fingers – mittens – are the way forward for both babies and toddlers. They are easy to put on and as long as they stay on, they'll be keeping your baby's hands warm while you're out and about.

**Cons:** Gloves with fingers are generally a waste of money for babies and toddlers – their fingers will never slide easily into the right finger space and you'll waste valuable minutes trying to sort it all out. Go for the mitten option – all you need to find is the thumb.

**What's it all about?** Make sure that any gloves you buy have Velcro or popper wrist fasteners in an attempt to keep them on Baby's hands. It's not such a bad idea to use a length of elastic to attach them to Baby's coat sleeves – yes, he or she will look a bit nerdy, but so what? It beats having to buy fourteen pairs of gloves every winter. As with hats, just because you don't tend to wear gloves doesn't mean that you should make that fashion choice for your little boy or girl – your fingers might be nice and toasty while you exercise your muscles pushing the pram, but poor little Baby is sat quite still in front of you and that cuttingly cold wind is chilling her exposed fingers fast.

**Bloke's Rating:** Essential, but impossible to keep on their hands. Expect to given 'the stare of hatred' by little old ladies looking at you for being such a cruel bastard when your baby has lost the umpteenth pair of gloves and is riding along in the pushchair with what could soon become a nasty dose of frostbite.

## Baby Leg-warmers

**Description:** A bit like tights that don't go all the way up. Think *Fame!* and you'll be on the right track. Baby leg warmers are lengths of material – usually horribly garish in appearance – that are worn on Baby's legs for protection against the cold, and protection against gravel and uneven surfaces when crawling. They make you dance better too. Put a pair of these on your child and she'll be pirouetting before she can walk in a straight line – well, maybe not, but it will be a lot less painful crawling round the garden.

**Pros:** Fashion statement aside, baby leg warmers will provide an extra layer of warmth whenever you are changing a nappy or Baby's clothes. Leg warmers are superb during those awkward spring and autumn months when it's not that warm and yet not cold enough to bring out the winter wear.

**Cons:** There are no two ways about it: your child will look daft wearing leg warmers. Maybe the world is wrong to judge a baby on his or her wardrobe, but the world will still judge and everyone knows a three-month-old can't buy things in shops, so they'll guess that the fashion freak must actually be you. If the guilt of making your child a fashion victim doesn't get you, remember that leg warmers are not tights and therefore there is nothing other than elastic keeping them up. If leg warmers become ankle warmers and Baby becomes positively obsessed with taking them off – you've only got yourself to blame.

**What's it all about?** The idea is sound, but they were obviously designed by someone who doesn't have kids and probably used to be a good but not a great dancer. It's hard enough to keep socks on a child, no matter what the age, and you've got shoes to help keep them strapped on. Leg warmers look good for about five seconds and then it all goes drastically wrong from there.

**Bloke's Rating:** I wanna live forever / I wanna learn how to wear trousers...

## Changing Bag

**Description:** A changing bag is a posh term for any large bag that you begin to use to cart around nappies, wipes, creams and all the other associated gubbins. If your partner chooses one it may well be 'baby themed', which means light pastel colours, embroidered bears or ducks, with lots of handy external pockets that only seem to be big enough to carry lipsticks and compact mirrors. If you choose the changing bag it will be unnecessarily large, probably black, and double as a rucksack. Either way you simply can't function as a parent on the move without one. Get shopping, before she does.

**Pros:** Assuming that you remember to replace empty packets of wipes, and there are always at least three nappies in the bag at any one time, your trips out of the house should always remain problem-free.

**Cons:** The changing bag soon becomes a general kit bag and briefcase. Every few months you will decide to sort out the nappy bag and inside you'll find every ballpoint pen you ever owned, two important letters that needed to be posted a week ago and some form of mushy fruit that's found its way into the workings of your mobile phone. The bigger the bag, the more useless rubbish you will end up carting around.

**What's it all about?** A changing bag will become your mobile life over the coming years and therefore it is important to ensure it has enough space for Baby's stuff and for your stuff. If you're a family that likes to do things at the weekend, ensure it's big enough for all of your partner's stuff too because, paradoxically, as the changing bag gets bigger, her handbag will get proportionally smaller. That's not a coincidence, nor is it just by chance that you get to carry it all the time. So, I stress again, if you're the one who will be lumbered with it you should be the one who chooses it.

**Bloke's Rating:** The beast-of-burden role will not end when your child is nappy-trained. Oh, no. Now you've got to exchange the nappy bag for a quite-capable-of-walking-by-herself toddler who wants to ride on Daddy's shoulders.

## Pushchair Bag

**Description:** If your pushchair doesn't have a built-in basket or netting underneath or if your Sherpa is off sick, it's time to invest in a pushchair bag. Just like your changing bag, the pushchair bag will soon be full of all the bits and bobs you need when you have a young child in a pram – apart from the obvious bum-changing stuff, you'll be carting round fruit, biscuits, used tissues, new tissues, toilet roll, random receipts, the odd pieces of paper and – let's not forget – the collection of empty wrappers that seem to find their way into every parent's bag. I don't even like Turkish Delight and neither do my children, so how did that wrapper end up there?

**Pros:** We all strive for extra space in every facet of life, in buying a house, a car or a pushchair bag. We can't get enough. The concept of maximum capacity is an ever-growing, non-achievable goal that seems to permeate the very fabric of existence. Manufacturers know this and that's why they will always be offering 'bigger and better' options. If size is what you're after, then size is what you'll get. Big and bold are so much better than small and pathetic – just ask your wife.

**Cons:** The more bags you have, the more likely it is you will fill them. No doubt if you decided to leave the house only armed with what you could fit into your breast pocket, you would get through the day unscathed, not missing a thing. Having said that, it is nice not to have to improvise everything and to have a few creature comforts like wipes and clean nappies.

**What's it all about?** At the end of the day, tying a plastic shopping bag to the handle of your pushchair will do exactly the same job, but the snob in all of us will shell out the extra money for something that looks attractive. When you've spent the best part of three hundred quid on the pushchair you're not going to spoil the look by compromising on accessories, are you?

**Bloke's Rating:** A bag is a bag, but you just can't help yourself, can you?

## Toddler Day-Sack

**Description:** There will come a time when you stop dead in your tracks. Maybe this is in the middle of a simple shopping trip, or as you reach down to find another slice of bread to throw to the ducks. You stop and for a moment you contemplate the amount of stuff you are carrying along with the baby. You've come out to buy two pints of milk, a Mars bar and a Saturday paper, yet you are carting around a changing bag full of gear, food and drink for the child, toys, a cuddly teddy and possibly a blanket and a dummy. This is to buy milk – not tackle the south face of Everest. What's going on? I'll tell you what's going on. The moment your child is walking; he or she is getting their own bag. Let him choose the bag, Postman Pat is good, or Bob or Thomas, it doesn't matter – as long as he carries it. Because once they're toddlers, it's payback time.

**Pros:** Letting your child carry some of the stuff that you need to bring out with you is not cruel, it's fair – assuming, of course, that you don't give him all the heavy stuff! Now Dad has a bag and Baby has a bag and together you can go shopping, or visit the aquarium or whatever – but you'll know that you are sharing the burden together. Even if your child is carrying some art supplies, a sandwich and a banana, the point is you are sharing the responsibility of going out, and after a few years of encouraging your child to share, you are finally able to reap the rewards.

**Cons:** Although your first-born will enjoy choosing a day-sack, and he might even make the right noises when you suggest that the sack is to be filled, not carried around empty, when it comes to the crunch you may be faced with a few tears when it becomes evident that the day-sack is not just an empty vessel put there for the sole purpose of collecting sticks, leaves and small rocks found on your walk. It's there for your son's food, drinks and toys. However, a few weeks down the line you'll find you've made the transition successfully. Suddenly Dad and Child have a bag each and although yours will be considerably heavier, you've successfully instilled a good lesson.

**What's it all about?** We all think the world of our kids and would do anything to make their lives easy and problem-free. However, life is no easy ride and although at first it may seem cruel, even at two or three years of age it's important to get children to help. Of course you could handle the extra weight of two apples, a piece of paper, a pen and a My Little Pony, but this is all about the principle of the matter.

**Bloke's Rating:** Sometimes we have to be cruel to be kind.

## Washing Machine

**Description:** Automated washing device for clothes, bedding and towels.

**Pros:** Laundrettes serve a purpose and for a single person or even a couple, they work. However, the one thing you will not have, once there is a baby in the family, is time. There are hardly enough hours in the day to get three meals on the table, so just when are you expecting to get the washing done? When you plan to visit the laundrette, baby will be asleep, upset or quite happy doing something else. A washing machine is an absolute necessity.

**Cons:** The detergents used in washing machines are killing fish and poisoning waterways, but the other option is washing by hand... Guess you don't care that much. Heavy use of washing machines will rack up your electricity bill and both washing powder and softeners aren't cheap, but then, neither are laundrettes and you don't have to walk half a mile with a bag full of your smelly socks.

**What's it all about?** A washing machine will lighten your load and that's a good thing – more time with your baby instead of with your laundry. The rule with washing machines is to buy the best that you can, given your circumstances. A better brand will pay off in the long run because you'll get a longer guarantee and the machine will be less likely to malfunction – saving you more in the long run. Always have your machine serviced.

**Bloke's Rating:** Plumb it in, turn it on and relax.

# Safety Equipment

Your home, sadly, is absolutely chock-full of dangers to babies and especially toddlers. Most rooms, for example, will have a number of power sockets at floor level and any electrical equipment will therefore have a very attractive cable dangling at about baby eye level. These cables will be pulled.

There is an essential process most parents go through once their baby is crawling and it's called 'toddler-proofing'. The sad fact of the matter is that no home is toddler-proof and it will be an ongoing responsibility for parents to maintain a vigilant eye. You can of course make your home safer, and the process of toddler-proofing is of paramount importance. Over the next few years lamps will be yanked off tables, stoves will be turned on and off, glasses and mugs will be knocked off counters and your stereo speakers will be painted in banana yoghurt. Despite this long five-

or-so-year war between your beautiful baby and your consumer electronics, you'll know you did your best.

In this chapter we will look at the many gadgets available to help make your home and environment safer for babies, but some common sense must also play a major part. Ensure there are no exposed electrical wires in or around the power sockets in your home. If your cooker has a large red on/off switch be sure to keep it off, rather than on, when you are not cooking. If you cannot live without your table lights, be sure to place the table flush with the wall so that the cable is trapped and you have a first line of defence against accidental falls. Bookshelves are incredibly handy for storing books but toddlers prefer to see them as climbing apparatus; if you can, remove these makeshift ladders from the rooms that your baby will be occupying during the day.

There are loads of products available to keep you, your baby and your home safe. Most of all be aware at all times of what your baby can reach and try to minimise their exposure to danger. Now, let's take a look at some of the gadgets available to help your child's early years remain accident-free.

## Cupboard Locks

**Description:** Cupboard locks are pretty self-explanatory. The number in a packet can vary, but what you get are simple plastic catches that attach to the inside or outside of cupboard doors to frustrate your child's obsession with laying his mitts on sharp, spiky things.

**Pros:** Although your child should feel the house belongs to them as much as it does to you, that should not include unauthorised access to bleach, weed-killer and fabric softener. Often these sorts of dangerous products are kept somewhere accessible in your home – under the kitchen sink, for example. A simple and cheap piece of plastic can ensure they don't get accidentally swallowed or poured on the floor.

**Cons:** There simply are no reasons why cupboard locks aren't a sensible purchase.

**What's it all about?** None of us wants to be parents who won't let our children explore, but there are limits. Sometimes you get to the point when you can no longer handle every pot and pan in the house being carried off and abandoned in the furthest part of the house. In most homes there is a 'bits' drawer or cupboard which holds essential items such as a measuring tape, spare batteries, a screwdriver or a ruler – can you find any of these items when you need them? No. And not just because the last person to use them hasn't returned them. If your little one gets access to this cupboard, then you may eventually find the contents in your shoes, or in the bin or jammed into the DVD player. Save yourself the aggro and fit a lock.

**Bloke's Rating:** Cheap and effective. Keeps unwanted fingers out.

## Plug Socket/Outlet Covers

**Description:** Plastic covers that fit into all of those plug sockets you have at toddler-level around the house. Why are plug sockets all at floor level? Why? Anyway, instead of offering your child three finger-sized holes that could lead to instant death in every corner of every room, they get to play with a blank piece of white plastic which is absolutely harmless. So, life for the little cherub is that much more safe, sterile and regulated – but that's a damn sight better than sending 220 volts through her arm.

**Pros:** Your child will stick her fingers into the power points. Once she's bored of sticking her fingers in there, she will start to use other objects – usually long skinny metal ones – and that's not an activity you really want to encourage.

**Cons:** None.

**What's it all about?** All those seventies' government adverts must have really rung true with us. We know electricity is dangerous. We may have even zapped ourselves by accident a couple of times. For minimal cost protect your little ones. There really is no excuse whatsoever.

**Bloke's Rating:** Don't play with electricity. It's not much fun.

## Sellotape For Your NTL/Sky Card

**Description:** OK, so Sellotape is hardly a funky gadget – there's probably already a roll in the house – but, if you are a household that enjoys Sky or any other cable or satellite television services, then chances are you have an attractive box sitting under the television that has a card poking out. That card is essential for your viewing pleasure. That card will be the first thing Baby removes and either a) hides or b) eats. Take the time to Sellotape the card to the box.

**Pros:** Sellotape is dirt-cheap. This essential job will take all of two minutes to complete. Avoid the inevitable hunting around the house for a chewed-up dog-eared piece of plastic. Guaranteed to work.

**Cons:** OK, so having Sellotape all over your audio visual altar right there in the front room for everyone to see can look a bit naff. It might even look like you took your Sky-Digibox out of someone else's bin, but you're a father now. Get over it. Trendy looks will just have to wait until the little one is not so little any more. Sorry.

**What's it all about?** Kids and consumer electronics do not mix. Your stereo, DVD player, VCR and anything else that is box-shaped and shiny is going to become very grubby, very soon. Don't be proud; be practical and get sticking.

**Bloke's Rating:** All too easy to ignore, all too easy to miss that all-important game on Sky Sports. All too easy to fix.

## VCR Lock

**Description:** A simple piece of plastic that is placed in the 'letter-box' of your VCR player to stop inquisitive fingers and non-video products being introduced to your VCR's sensitive heads.

**Pros:** For a few pounds you will be able to insert this plastic protector into your VCR and not have to worry about little gifts of buttery toast, forks, pencils, socks or coins being 'posted' into the workings.

**Cons:** There aren't really many cons to this device. OK, so it looks a bit naff and the colour will never be exactly the same as your VCR, but really it is far cheaper than having to replace the whole thing or paying to have it fixed. Slightly older children may feel put out that they have to ask you to remove the shield before they can use the video, but that's not such a big deal.

**What's it all about?** Simple and effective, the VCR lock will save you money. The trick is to remember to insert it after you've finished watching a video. Every time. One slip and it's a waste of money!

**Bloke's Rating:** Invest in your continued audio/visual pleasure.

## Shelving

**Description:** Not strictly a gadget, but installing some shelves will help protect your electronic and most precious gadgets from the loving but often destructive hands of your child. Buy ready-made shelves or customise your room by making your own.

**Pros:** The maxim 'Out of sight, out of mind' is especially true for kids and therefore you've only got yourself to blame if you notice your toddler has taken an interest in your new DVD recorder and you fail to move it before the inevitable accident.

**Cons:** You have probably already purchased a beautiful stand for your television, which, before kids came along, displayed your consumer electronics to exquisite advantage. But don't worry, we're not saying it'll go to waste – far from it. Now you have kiddie-sized shelves they can use for soggy biscuits, melting Cadbury's Buttons and pieces of banana. Fab, hey?

**What's it all about?** Unless you have a very big home indeed, it's impossible, and a wee bit Fascist, to keep children out of certain rooms of the house. Therefore, if they're allowed in you can't be surprised if a few accidents happen... build or buy some shelves and get everything up high. Note that this is a never-ending process – our daughter is now five, and, we thought, trustworthy around consumer electronics. My new funky flat-screen computer monitor is only ten days old as I write this and already there's a pen scratch across the screen – not an ink stain that can be wiped away, but an actual ten-inch gash. Nice. What can you do?

**Bloke's Rating:** Generally shelves do look naff and they're a pain to assemble, but sometimes it's the only way.

## Table Corner Guards

**Description:** Plastic or foam pads that are placed over the corners of toddler-height tables. The pads usually have an adhesive underside for easy application. Although corner guards won't stop your child bumping into things, they will protect his head, face and arms from any nasty bumps and bruises. They might actually stop you hurting your shin every now and again too.

**Pros:** Being a baby or a toddler is hard work. There's so much to see and do but their legs don't necessarily do what they should. The body is travelling in one direction but there's an interesting bit of plastic over in the far corner and – what happens? The baby loses what little balance he has, most likely when he was right next to a table corner.

**Cons:** Corner guards are without exception ugly and very obvious. They do make your fancy coffee table, or glass TV-stand look rubbish, but it's a price you will have to pay.

**What's it all about?** Add the corner guards before your child is even crawling, and when he is not in the room – otherwise the new sudden addition to the room will become a focal point and Baby might begin a campaign of removal, resulting in your corner guards being peeled off and losing their stickiness.

**Bloke's Rating:** Function over form, Dad.

## Hearth-/Fireguard

**Description:** A hearth- or fireguard is a metal barrier which can vary in shape and weight, and simply acts as a barrier between red-hot coals or burning wood and your exploring child. Those of you lucky enough to still have a real fire in your home can sit there smug and content; that is, until little fingers decide to play with the coal bucket and, after your darling child has covered his hands in coal dust, he decides to climb on your new cream leather sofa...

**Pros:** Anyone with a real fire should have a hearth-guard anyway, otherwise hot embers are likely to be spat out and make a nice burn mark on your carpet. With kids in the equation too, it just makes common sense. Be sure to keep your fire-building material and the associated poker, brush, pan etc. behind the guard too.

**Cons:** Hearth-guards tend to be quite small and although they will stop flying embers from igniting your carpet, they won't do a lot to stop the impact of a toddler. They can also be quite small and therefore your toddler can simply crawl or walk around them to get to the danger area. The solution? Well, you could get rid of your open fire, but that would be a bit extreme. What we did was to buy three cheap hearth-guards and link them all together with carabiners (metal rings with a latch) and then fix the two end guards to the wall. A bit of an effort, and there's now an awful lot of metalwork in our front room, but we get the benefit of a wood-stove without the worry of a trip to the burns unit. After baby bedtime, the barriers are detached from the wall and folded up out of the way. Yes, it adds maybe five minutes of fiddling before we can sit down and gaze at the fire, but who cares.

**What's it all about?** Once again this is all about practicality over the subtler points of interior design. As we look at each of the gadgets available to us it becomes ever more clear that the safer you make your home, the worse it will look.

**Bloke's Rating**: Don't play with fire. Buy a fireguard.

## Baby/Stair Gate

**Description:** A wooden or metal gate that is fixed to the wall at the top or bottom of the stairs in your house to stop nasty falls or exploratory climbs. Stair gates can be fixed to the wall with screws or adjustable pressure bolts – both are reasonably easy to put into place. The screw-on version will obviously involve drilling holes, which may not be an option if you live in rented accommodation. We found this out after the event and got a very nasty letter from the landlord – nothing a bit of Polyfilla couldn't fix, but that argument didn't seem to wash and the 'damage' was docked from our deposit.

**Pros:** The obvious advantage of fixing a stair gate is that you don't need to have eyes in the back of your head every minute of every day. There are occasions when you'll be on the phone, or on the loo, or cooking, when your toddler is pottering around quite happily. It only takes a second for them to be off on their first unaccompanied ascent and that's what you want to stop. Stair gates are also a great way to demarcate which areas of the house are primarily for Baby to roam and which bits, depending on the layout of your home, are primarily for Mum and Dad to enjoy without having to worry too much about wiping up any spilt orange juice before they sit down.

**Cons:** It can seem rather cruel to put up bars in your home. Although it's easy for you to climb over, or open and close the gate when you wish – that boundary and that forbidden fruit of life on the other side will be a constant focus for your toddler. Stair gates get some serious abuse and if a child is persistent enough can be literally ripped from their brackets, but usually by that stage the child is pretty good on stairs and you can always encourage them to help fix the holes in the wall. Stair gates can be frustrating for older children in the house, especially if the locking mechanism is quite complex. You might find that you are forever opening and closing the gate to let the older child in and out, which just adds to your toddler's frustration at being penned in. Still, having a stair gate is better than not.

**What's it all about?** Stair gates aren't just for stairs. You might find that after your baby has turned into a child and is pretty careful on the stairs you'll have other uses for stair gates – usually on the outside of a bedroom door. About the time that you move your child from a cot to a bed, you may also find that bedtimes aren't as straightforward as they once were. Now you put your child into bed and he follows you out of the room. You can't shut the door because he wants the light from the hall and you can't leave the door open because he'll trot downstairs, get on the sofa and look bewildered when you explain that CBeebies has finished transmitting and no, you wouldn't prefer to watch *The Tweenies* on DVD.

**Bloke's Rating:** Pen them in. They can do what they like when they turn eighteen, but until then it's your house and your rules!

## Stair Netting

**Description:** A length of netting that is attached to either the banister of your staircase, or, if you have one, the railings of your balcony or terrace. The netting is there to stop your toddler launching missiles at your own, or some other unsuspecting person's, head.

**Pros:** Stair netting works, assuming that the gaps are small enough. The 'hilarious' game of posting things through the balustrades is fine, up to a point, but when it's Mum or Dad's job to collect and return said item, the novelty wears off quickly for parents. If you've been running down three floors, popping outside and hunting on a busy road for Baby's favourite rattle, then you'll have already installed stair netting.

**Cons:** The netting can and usually does look a bit rubbish, especially on an internal staircase. There is a temptation for kids to pull themselves up or even to try and climb on the netting – be aware of this when you are first fixing it. Try, if you can, to keep as much of it as possible out of reach.

**What's it all about?** Most importantly, balcony owners should bear in mind that you would most likely be held responsible if something was launched from a balcony and it injured someone below. This could end in an expensive court case. And sprinting up and down those stairs to retrieve toys and stop your baby howling really is a complete pain in the arse.

**Bloke's Rating:** For balconies it's a must.

## Temperature Monitor / Thermometer

**Description:** A device for reading the temperature of you or your baby. One simple thermometer comes as a stick to be placed in the mouth or under the armpit. Digital thermometers are also available and are usually inserted into the ear.

**Pros:** It is very worrying, as a parent, when your child is obviously hot and bothered. A thermometer will confirm that, and depending on the reading, you can make an informed decision about what to do next. A high temperature can be very dangerous and should be monitored. Thermometers are reasonably cheap and I think they are an essential for every home.

**Cons:** I've used a couple of different types of ear thermometers over the last few years and, whilst I think that they are all very useful and a necessary thing to have in the house, what worries me is that you can take three readings from the same ear in the space of a minute and get varying results. One temperature reading could mean the boy is burning, the second could mean he got a bit hot and flustered watching *Teletubbies*, and the third reading means that he is completely fine. How can you know that the result is a true representation of the seriousness of the situation? The answer is to treat the results from an ear thermometer as a guide only. If the result is consistently high, then you can safely assume your child has a fever, although placing your hand on their forehead will tell you this as well!

**What's it all about?** Kids don't have the same fine-tuned immune system as you and therefore contract illnesses far more often and can't fight them off as quickly as a grown-up can. There will be occasions when you will need to take your child to the doctor because of a hot forehead and the doctor will appreciate a log of what temperatures you have recorded and when.

**Bloke's Rating:** Better safe than sorry. Measure, record and administer Calpol.

## Reins

**Description:** You have two options: the chest reins that are worn over baby clothes with a lead for Dad to hold onto, or the wrist attachment for older children which allows Dad to gently coax Child to walk in the right direction.

**Pros:** Some parents argue that the reins are particularly useful when Baby is taking those first early steps – that extra bit of help from Dad stops Baby falling over all the time. The reins are there to help balance, not imprison. Mmmm. Not sure. Some children really do run in random directions all of the time. If this is the case, then using reins and allowing your child to walk is far preferable to pushing them around in a pushchair all the time.

**Cons:** Looks – and probably feels to your child – as though you are walking a dog, not your own flesh and blood.

**What's it all about?** Roads are lethal and although we all try to instil a fear and respect of traffic into children, they are easily distracted and, as we all know, can just run off when you least expect it. Reins are a somewhat severe way to minimise the risk.

**Bloke's Rating:** Personally I would just let your child walk around without reins – as long as they are holding your hand or the pushchair.

# R & R

As you will soon find out, babies spend a tremendous amount of time sleeping. Sadly their schedule is unlikely to be similar to yours, at least not for the first couple of months anyway. While it is true that most babies will sleep absolutely anywhere, you will want to establish the habit of putting baby to 'bed' when they're tired, and that means buying a cot.

Very soon, however, your baby is not a baby any more and you will need to buy a bed and update the nursery into a suitable bedroom for your toddler. As well as the essential sleeping apparatus, there's a whole raft of equipment just waiting in retail outlets across the land that has your baby's name on it.

We all appreciate the benefits of rest and a comfortable environment. Now is the time to look at all of the gadgets on the market to make your life and the life of your baby as relaxing as they possibly could be.

## Moses Basket

**Description:** A Moses basket is a wicker carrier for newborn babies, named after the crib made of reeds in which the baby Moses was apparently found. Some parents prefer the Moses basket to a cot for the early weeks because it is a little more enclosed, and after being in a womb for nine months, Baby is likely to be a bit surprised at all that empty space. The Moses basket will keep your baby warm and secure and the handles mean that Mum and Dad can move Baby from room to room when they need to – without disturbing her.

**Pros:** As well as being portable, some Moses baskets come with a stand so that baby can be raised to bed height, which both gives easy access for Mum and Dad and means they can look over at their newborn and admire him without getting out from under the duvet. The close sides of the Moses basket may mean your baby sleeps better in the early weeks.

**Cons:** Your newborn will only be newborn for a very short period of time; before you feel like you've caught your breath after the birth, they're suddenly a few months old and far too long for the Moses basket. Moses baskets are expensive and this limited lifespan is a real disadvantage. Starting a baby in a basket and then upgrading to a cot can cause a few sleep problems when you make the switch, because baby is unsettled by a change in his sleeping environment. Some parents insist on bypassing the problem by putting baby in their cot, right from day one.

**What's it all about?** There's something quite cute and traditional about Moses baskets, that means many new parents will buy one without really thinking about it. Although new babies look tiny and vulnerable in a cot, it won't be long until they grow into it.

**Bloke's Rating:** Nice, as long as someone else buys it.

## Crib

**Description:** A crib is somewhere in between a Moses basket and a cot. Just like a basket, it offers Baby a more enclosed environment but its extra length will mean it lasts for about six months instead of six weeks. Usually made of wood, cribs tend to be very beautiful and seem fitting for your pride and joy.

**Pros:** Most cribs either glide or rock; this gentle movement can be a great help when you want Baby to sleep, but Baby has got other ideas. The raised structure of the crib is useful when you are putting Baby to sleep and retrieving her when she's awake.

**Cons:** The fancy looks and the swinging action are all very well, but you're eventually going to have to upgrade to a cot, and, just as with the Moses basket, there can a period of disapproval from your baby when you decide to make that switch. Cribs are big and bulky, so you won't be able to cart Baby around the house in one of these; wherever you erect it is where it is going to stay.

**What's it all about?** Whenever we picture a nursery, in the mind's eye, there's usually a crib in it — that feeling that they are the norm can be a difficult one to ignore and many a parent has opted for a crib even though they can scant afford it.

**Bloke's Rating:** Choose a Moses basket or a crib if you must, but don't buy both.

## Cots

**Description:** Cots come in a variety of shapes and sizes and a mind-boggling range of prices. What you are buying is four wooden panels and a mattress – a sleeping area for baby, that stops them from falling or climbing out. Cots are good from birth onwards and, whatever price you pay, you will get your money's worth.

**Pros:** Cots nowadays are robust, strong and resilient. You may wonder what damage your little angel could possibly inflict on such a large wooden structure, but it's only a matter of months before Baby turns into Toddler and with that important stage in development comes your child's ability to hit, kick, rage and throw themselves about. When this anger and frustration take place within the confines of a cot you'll realise just why they are so chunky and strong.

**Cons:** Starting Baby sleeping in a cot from birth can be a bit of a shock for them – all that exposed space is daunting and there may well be a few tears and some long, long bedtimes – but you will manage, eventually. Look to buy a cot which has drop-down sides, as this will make it far easier on your bad back when it comes to picking Baby up out of the cot.

**What's it all about?** A word of warning: if you do decide to buy a second-hand cot, be sure to wash it thoroughly before use and under no circumstances should you use the original mattress – used mattresses have been linked with cot-death. This rule is equally true if the cot was used by one of your own children. Buy a new mattress! When it comes to buying a cot, if you bear in mind that Baby is soon going to grow up and need his own bed, you might consider a cot/bed. As the name suggests it's a cot until you take the sides off and then it is transformed into a junior bed. A great way to save some cash.

**Bloke's Rating:** The single most important gadget you can buy.

## Bouncing/Vibrating Chair

**Description:** A colourful sun-lounger rigged up to a battery pack to shake, rattle and roll your baby to sleep. It may sound and look a bit basic and it is, but this simple device can give whoever has been carrying the little one for the last hour and a half a welcome break and a chance for their arm and back to recover.

**Pros:** New babies like to feel secure, all the time. After nine months of floating in amniotic fluid with the steady beat of a mother's heart and constant warmth and darkness, the outside world can be a harsh and unwelcoming place for the little one. The net effect is that one of you will need to hold your baby constantly. Now, although a vibrating chair won't replace the womb, the gentle movement, comfortable reclining position and safety belt will all make Baby feel that much more secure, buying Mum or Dad the chance to prepare a meal, go to the loo or just take a short break from being a load-bearing donkey for a few minutes. Babies often go to sleep on the chair. In later months the chair can prove invaluable when you're first starting to spoon-feed. If your child has become used to sitting in the chair, the introduction of solids will be less of a shock than if you are also introducing the wonders of a new high chair. If there are other siblings in the house, strap your baby in and let little brothers and sisters amuse and interact with your baby. The chair also allows Baby safely to observe what's going on in a room, even if that's just you getting dressed in the morning.

**Cons:** The vibrating chair does not cut the mustard with every baby. As with all things, it becomes expensive buying gadgets that your baby doesn't like or use, and there's no real way of testing that until you've bought it and brought it home. Within seconds it will be covered in sick and you're stuck with it.

**What's it all about?** The vibrating chair is all about giving you another option for short periods during the day when you can get on with other things whilst keeping an eye on your little one. If Baby likes it, it's a fantastic investment. If she doesn't, it's just more clutter for your home.

## Sleeping Bags / Grobags

**Description:** Bringing the great outdoors into the comfort of your home. Actually, that's not true. Sleeping bags for babies are the straightforward solution to keeping your baby warm in her cot. No matter how well you cover your baby with sheets, babies turn and wriggle so much that inevitably the covers end up in a discarded pile in one corner of the cot and Baby wakes up incredibly cold in another. The sleeping bag option means that they are kept warm by their own body heat all night, no matter how much they move.

**Pros:** Sleeping bags are inexpensive compared to good-quality blankets and you only really need to have two. I recommend that you buy two the same, so that there aren't any problems in later months when Baby learns to prefer one to the other. Having two identical bags also means that you can wash one when necessary and not have to resort to sheets again.

**Cons:** The sleeping bags tend not to offer any protection for Baby's arms so on cold nights you may have to put a long-sleeve top on your baby so that they don't get chilly.

**What's it all about?** Using a sleeping bag, especially when your child has become mobile, is a great way to prevent any cot escapes. The sleeping bag does make it difficult for Baby to move freely, but the point of putting them in the cot is to get them to sleep, not stretch their legs and jump up and down. Baby can still turn, wriggle and grow and all the time keep snug and warm. Be sure to buy the right thickness of sleeping bag for the seasons in which she will be using it.

**Bloke's Rating:** Brilliant – simple but effective.

## Sleep Music

**Description:** Sleep music can be useful for you as well as for Baby. Sometimes we all need a bit of assistance getting to sleep. There's obviously lots of kiddie-specific material available, but nursery rhymes can stimulate rather than relax, and the tried-and-tested material seems to be more along the lines of either gentle instrumentals or new-age stuff featuring a porpoise singing and such like.

**Pros:** We are all affected by the tempos and noises that

surround us in life – be they traffic, sirens, chatter from the street or the general noises from within the house like the humming fridge and the washing-machine spin cycle. Babies are attuned to these tempos too, and therefore it is sometimes necessary to encourage a change of pace, especially if it's time for Baby to have a nap. By playing relaxing sleep music you can force a time change and help your son or daughter relax – assuming you've put the correct CD in and the volume is not set to max.

**Cons:** Obviously, if your mates see that whale-song CDs and the pan-pipe albums have materialised in your collection, then, naturally, they're going to get a bit worried about you. Hide them if you must.

**What's it all about?** The sound of a blue whale mating or the call of the happy dolphins leading yachts into Melbourne harbour are regarded so highly by some people that a multi-million pound business has grown despite most people's scepticism.

**Bloke's Rating:** Don't worry – buying a new-age CD won't lead you down the rocky road of wearing tie-dye clothing and banging bongos of an evening. Not unless you want it to, that is.

## Mobile

**Description:** One of the first decorations or stimulants you will buy for your baby after his or her first cuddly toy will be the mobile to hang above the cot. Mobiles can either dangle from the ceiling or else come with a bracket with which they can be attached to the cot. A mobile usually has little pieces of plastic, card or fabric dangling from a central frame which gently turns and spins with the movement of air within a room, or by a quiet motor.

**Pros:** There's no denying that if you stick a mobile up above the head of a baby they will stare intently and their eyes will follow every movement. I'm sure you could make you own, but that would look a bit tacky, really.

**Cons:** The cot-mounted mobiles are attractive, thus we buy them, but come the day when baby is standing, or pulling himself up using the cot as support, the mobile will be ripped off and used as a makeshift percussion instrument or a missile. The ceiling-mounted mobile will last longer, but when your newborn's eyes are first adjusting and focusing on this brave new world, it could be far too far away to be appreciated.

**What's it all about?** For very young babies the experts recommend black-and-white mobiles – babies seem to appreciate the stark contrast much more than looking at primary colours, or, worse, pastels.

**Bloke's Rating:** Get the stepladder out and get climbing – Baby's room isn't complete until there's something dangling from the ceiling.

## Plug-in Night Light

**Description:** A small low-power light that you can plug into a socket so that your child isn't going to sleep in complete darkness or so that there is a bit of light to guide your infant to the loo or your bedroom in the middle of the night.

**Pros:** Although very young babies don't mind complete

darkness, as children begin to get older they have dreams and nightmares and start wondering if Sully or Randall are hiding in their cupboard. Then they start asking for you to leave the door open and the landing light on. The plug-in night light is the answer. Rather than keeping the whole house lit up, this little beauty emits just enough light to comfort your child without affecting their sleep – or your own. As they get to an age when they start wandering around at night, and especially if they have to pass or use the staircase, the night light can be strategically placed to avoid any nasty falls.

**Cons:** None. Although you would prefer it if they slept without a light, if they say they want a light, then you will most probably go ahead and buy one.

**What's it all about?** Keeping the peace and making bedtime as stress-free for all concerned as you can.

**Bloke's Rating:** Cheap and effective.

## Lamp With Revolving Shade

**Description:** Lamps for kids usually come with a revolving shade that projects images on to the wall of their bedroom. Quite often their favourite cartoon characters are depicted and a beautiful ballet ensues as the heat from the bulb causes the shade to revolve.

**Pros:** Most kids like some kind of light on in their room when they are going to sleep, so the lamp has obvious appeal and the revolving shade does help relax their mind. Some lamps come with an on/off switch as part of the cable and if the light is left on a bedside table, you can begin to teach your child the importance of turning the light off when they are ready to go to sleep. The flipside of this of course is that they can turn the light on again easily if you have switched it off – but that's part of the game, isn't it?

**Cons:** Often the shade is delicately balanced on a small pin so that it can turn easily – the downside of this is that you or your child will be forever knocking the shade off the pin and they're tricky to put back on, especially if you've just turned the light off and you are trying to sneak out of the bedroom when your child is asleep.

**What's it all about?** Some parents worry about leaving a lamp near their child's bed, in case little hands make contact with the hot bulb. There is always that risk and usually the shade completely envelops the bulb, so that the rising heat can turn the shade. There is also a time when you must start accepting that their bedroom is fraught with danger with or without a lamp – just look how many power sockets are in there. At least the lamp plugs one of those up. Kids enjoy a bit of autonomy and the option to turn their own lamp on and off can be a real defining moment in their development.

**Bloke's Rating:** A firm favourite in our house.

## Cot-Side Music Box / Light Show

**Description:** A music box is a common sight for younger babies in cots. Wind it up just as you are putting Baby to bed and for a few minutes the box will play a gentle lullaby, helping Baby get off to sleep.

**Pros:** Most music boxes are hand-wound, which means the

music slowly comes to a stop rather than abruptly switching off – something which might wake Baby up. Most music boxes have an inbuilt light which sends a projection on to the wall or the ceiling. The volume of the music box is loud enough to be soothing but not enough to startle or scare.

**Cons:** When Baby gets a bit older and wakes in the morning she will learn to wind the box herself so that the whole house can wake up to the *Winnie The Pooh* theme tune, but that's kind of cute.

**What's it all about?** Once you have a music box it becomes part of the bedtime routine – reassuring for Baby, especially if she associates it with drifting peacefully off to sleep.

**Bloke's Rating:** Life without a music box wouldn't feel right.

## Playhouse

**Description:** Whether it is made of material and bought through a catalogue or whether it is lovingly custom-built out of stripped pine by Dad, the playhouse is the ultimate admission that your kids have taken over. Never mind your plans for growing rare and exotic grasses. Never mind the subtle but interesting planting pattern you planned with the tulips and the daffodils. None of that matters any more. You have kids and they are going to colonise your garden in much the same style that the British Empire commanded the four corners of the earth. Don't even bother with the rare and the hard-to-grow – the ground will be so trampled it will be a wonder if the lawn survives.

**Pros:** Encouraging independent thought is absolutely essential when it comes to rearing kids. There will of course be occasions when we want our children to act the way we would act, given the same situation, but you know that they won't. Having a playhouse allows kids' imaginations to run riot. Hours of fun can be had in a playhouse and that's good news for parent and child.

**Cons:** Other than the prohibitive cost of some playhouses, nothing at all.

**What's it all about?** When we were kids we would actually build a playhouse and call it a den. We didn't buy it in kit form and we certainly wouldn't want to build a den in our own garden or backyard – part of the buzz and appeal was building a sustainable shelter in the middle of the woods. I'm not sure what has changed over the last two or three decades – maybe it's nothing – but something inside me says it is now far more dangerous for my son or daughter to play alone in the woods than it was for me to do the same thing. The solution? The den is now in the back garden.

**Bloke's Rating:** Although the pressure will be on to buy a 'ready-made' playhouse, there is something to be said for encouraging your child to build a shelter from the materials available: under your direction, of course. A bivouac created from fallen logs and ferns can be an incredibly comfortable and warm shelter, but if none of that is to hand, then a large sheet of tarpaulin will do.

## Play Tent

**Description:** A small tent, usually with a cartoon character pattern, for use indoors or outside if it is warm and dry.

**Pros:** Play tents work in the same way as playhouses – loads of fun for Baby, going in and out of the tent with a collection of toys and plastic tea-making facilities. No real idea about what keeps them so amused for so long, but the tent works its magic and that's all that matters, really. Children's imaginations are often their best friend.

**Cons:** Although your son will be more than happy to fill the tent with every toy he owns along with random items found throughout the house, when it comes to clearing the tent out at the end of the day, then the responsibility will be left to you. Your son won't want to know. Great.

**What's it all about?** A play tent is perfect for encouraging independent and imaginative play. Your child knows you are close by but also enjoys the privacy of 'hiding' away.

**Bloke's Rating:** Lots of fun.


## Bubble Machine

**Description:** Fed up with buying pots and pots of bubble mix only to find that a) it's all been tipped out on the floor or b) it doesn't work very well or c) your child hasn't got enough puff and just gets frustrated? Well, help is at hand in the form of a bubble machine. Put in the batteries, add the 'magic water' and turn it on – thousands of bubbles fill the sky and all the children are enraptured.

**Pros:** The pleasure that bubbles give is immense. Children are a joy to watch most of the time, but when they are trying to burst bubbles or caress one without popping it, it really is quite special. Let's be honest, bubbles are quite pretty and you won't be the first father to stick the Bubble Machine on in the privacy of your own home with just you and the wife there to watch. You know, just to check it works.

**Cons:** Only the apparently constant need for new batteries – best to get rechargeable.

**What's it all about?** Bubbles, bubbles, bubbles. Lots of them. A bubble machine is far cheaper than a kid's entertainer for birthday parties and will probably mean more fun for the little one – just watch out for those slippery floors after prolonged use.

**Bloke's Rating:** Has been successfully used as a pacifier for our over-excited kids.

## Art Easel

**Description:** A wooden or plastic A-frame with a white- or blackboard or plain front. Some come with a dowel on the top so you can roll down a new sheet of paper, others have a combination of drawing surfaces. Most easels have a storage shelf which can be used to secure paints, brushes, paper and colouring pens.

**Pros:** Kids love art and having an easel will save your kitchen table from any more abuse. Kids don't seem to mind standing up to paint or draw, and using an easel seems to really open up the full size and potential of the canvas as opposed to table drawings, which are often small and concentrated in one corner of the paper.

**Cons:** Easels are quite bulky and although they often fold up they still need to go away somewhere. That somewhere is already full to the brim with everything else you and your children own. Early experimentation with paint and water may result in lots of messy drips, so best to set up the art school in a room that doesn't have a carpeted floor.

**What's it all about?** Whatever your feelings on the subject, it is important to remember that art is as important a subject as literature or biology – encouraging your child to be artistic and creative will set them up for pre-school and school, and help with their communication.

**Bloke's Rating:** Lots of fun for you and the kids. Why don't you give the easel a go too? You may surprise yourself – and if it's really rubbish, you can say your two-year-old did it!

# Height Chart

**Description:** A length of wood or plastic that you pin or nail to the wall, usually in the shape of a giraffe or other long creature that has measurements running along the side. Shop at the top end of the market and you will get little spring-loaded markers to move up and down the height chart mapping your child's progress from the floor – or you can use a biro.

**Pros:** As blokes we're pretty much obsessed with the biggest, longest, widest – and that obsession transfers to our kids. There was nothing so cringeworthy for a boy to hear as the words 'Last time I saw you, you were only this tall' – and yet, secretly, we basked in the glory. Well, it's the same for your kids, and they are going to want to measure their height pretty often, and sometimes get confused about why they haven't grown since lunchtime.

**Cons:** None. Height charts are limited to about 1 meter 40 cm, but once your child is this tall they're unlikely to want to have a wooden giraffe hanging from the wall.

**What's it all about?** Height charts are great for brightening up a child's room, and for the first couple of weeks when you put up a height chart your child will want to be measured a couple of times an hour, to see how much they've grown. As the weeks go by this begins to settle down a bit.

**Bloke's Rating:** My three-year-old is taller than yours...

## Musical Instruments

**Description:** Music is one of the purest forms of artistic expression. Whether you agree with that statement or not will depend entirely on how many times you have heard every saucepan, table and fridge door being beaten with a wooden spoon over the course of the last twelve months. Despite the improvised soundscapes that have amused both you and your neighbours, you'll still feel the need – or at least your friends and family will feel the need – to start purchasing either a glockenspiel or, if you're a little bit more adventurous and rich, Baby's first grand piano.

**Pros:** Children are either turned on or off by music appreciation, or, more importantly, music making, from a very early age.

**Cons:** Introducing a number of musical instruments to a child will not result in an overnight child prodigy. Far from it. You will of course be setting yourself and your partner up for what you may feel to be a lifetime of scales, missed notes and amateur performances at school concerts. That's not to say that your child's effort, or your expense, is wasted.

Far from it – if they can continue during the 'wilderness years' and come out the other side of puberty still interested and still playing, then you and they are onto a good thing, and your son or daughter will have a career which they can follow, or at least a satisfying hobby.

**What's it all about?** Making music is fun but it will be a very long time before you as a parent will hear anything that actually resembles music.

**Bloke's Rating:** Tambourine, yes; full drum kit... probably not.

# Cleaning and Maintenance

Kids are dirty creatures. Yes, they're cute and cuddly and all the rest of it, but the state they can get into in a matter of minutes will continue to surprise you for years and years. All they need is one chance, one lapse of concentration on your part, and it's carnage. Absolute-bloody-horror, and if they're anywhere near a squeezy-bottle of tomato ketchup at the time, then it really will look like bloody horror.

You'll forgive them, eventually, but it will be an emotional couple of minutes as you waste an entire kitchen roll or a packet of wipes cleaning up the damage that some puréed pears can reap upon your home and more specifically your upholstery, jumper and the hall, stairs and landing carpet.

Being a dad is all about being the maid. You've just cleaned up and no one in the house wants to keep the place tidy – even for ten minutes. You feel like you're wasting your time, no one appreciates the role you are playing and the time you've spent mopping up was totally wasted, because the house looks like a team of hoodie-wearing youths have been squatting in your lounge for the best part of a month and your partner only went to see her friend for two hours. 'What happened?' you are asked. With a look of abject confusion you raise an accusatory finger at the eighteen-month-old grinning in the pit of carnage that was once your living room...

Thankfully help is on hand. It won't stop the mess – kids are too good, even for these gadgets. But they might go some way to making the experience of looking after a baby or toddler a little bit easier.

## Disposable Nappies

**Description:** Some might say this is the easy, selfish option. They might even be right. Disposable nappies are the standard ones that you can buy from any supermarket or corner shop in the country. Shaped to wrap around Baby's bum and to stick together with minimal-fuss Velcro, disposable nappies are strong, absorbent and comfortable to wear – at least, that's what I understand. I haven't tried wearing one myself.

**Pros:** When it comes to dealing with your child's poo, you really want to be shot of the foul stuff as quickly as possible. The disposable nappy facilitates this. Pull off the tabs, remove the offending article, a quick wipe of the bum, a new nappy on, and bingo! you're back in business. Until the next time.

**Cons:** It is a given that disposable nappies are a massive environmental problem. The reality, for most parents, is that it is better to have a long-term environmental problem than tolerate your child's poo being in the room with you any longer than necessary.

**What's it all about?** It can be either an emotive, tricky subject or you can categorically decide from the outset that you couldn't care less and you are going to buy and use disposable nappies right from the get go. Either way, you won't be alone. The vast majority of parents use disposable nappies and will continue to do so. Moral and ecological arguments aside, you will choose which nappy route to take very early on, and stick to that decision. Be realistic about how much time you have on any given day and then make your choice.

**Bloke's Rating:** I don't want to take the moral high ground or low ground with this book and therefore I have to admit to being a fan of disposable nappies because they suit our circumstances. We do care about the environment, the current state of world peace, poverty, Third-World debt and who shot JR, but we are also realists living in a capitalist society at the turn of the 21st century. We use disposable nappies and will continue to do so until our son is potty-trained. Our carbon footprint on the world is probably a contributory factor to other people's suffering. For that I am sorry. But my son has got a clean bum and all is well with us. Selfish? Yes, very, but I'm man enough to admit it. If it's any consolation we do our bit by recycling plastics, bottles and tin cans. So should you.

## Biodegradable Disposable Nappies

**Description:** The same as above only you won't be hurting the environment quite so much.

**Pros:** There's no pretending that even biodegradable nappies will dissolve away in a matter of days or even weeks. The reality of course is that it will take years for the nappies to completely return to the earth. However, compared to normal disposable nappies, this process is infinitely quicker and therefore if you are any way inclined to think or vote Green, then you should be looking at biodegradable nappies. Despite your fears, biodegradable nappies aren't any less absorbent or in any way inferior to ordinary nappies.

**Cons:** There's an associated cost to biodegradable nappies that you will really notice over the course of your child's early years. That cost may not have an impact on the environment, but it will on your wallet. Availability can sometimes be an issue if you're not near a supermarket, but there are a number of websites where you can buy biodegradable nappies. See Useful Contacts at the back of the book. Also note that only about 70% of the components in biodegradable nappies actually do degrade quickly; the remaining 30% of materials take hundreds of years, just like regular disposable nappies... Sleep well tonight, won't you?

**What's it all about?** Biodegradable nappies give you a chance to be ethical in your choice of nappies, although terry nappies, even taking into account the amount of detergent used over a three-year period, are without a doubt the most eco-friendly option.

**Bloke's Rating:** Be as ecologically friendly as your wallet allows.

## Towel/Terry Nappies – Basic

**Description:** You probably wore these when you were a lad. Proper nappies. Lengths of towelling wrapped around a baby to catch any and all excretions. This is what people used before disposable nappies ever existed. It's the purists' choice.

**Pros:** Although the initial outlay is quite high because it's recommended that you have at least two dozen, once you've bought them, that's it. You will never run out of nappies and you will never have to buy any more. In a nutshell, you'll save about £700 a year, per baby, for two to three years. That's over £2,000, or a 42-inch HD-ready plasma-screen television. Nappies are a blight on the environment. Not just a little bit of a problem but an enormous mountain of non-biodegradable waste that will continue to fester in landfill sites around the world, probably to the end of time. Everyone knows cockroaches will probably be the only survivors of a nuclear holocaust. Used nappies will be their nuclear-winter homes.

**Cons:** You have to learn nappy origami in order to convert that square of terry cloth into something wearable, and you're always at risk of spiking your son and daughter with a giant safety pin. Oh, and there's the poo. Lots of poo. Lots of washing too. If you didn't have enough on your plate already, you'll be adding the rather unfortunate daily grind of removing poo and washing heavily-soiled nappies. It's not going to make your life any easier. Or much more fun. Thankfully, you can invest in nappy liners, which means that you can pick up the poo in the removable lining and flush it all away down the loo – far easier and far less messy.

**What's it all about?** It's decision time. Both the environmental and the financial arguments are obviously in favour of using towel nappies, but the reality of being cash-rich, time-poor wage slaves is that most of us choose to stick two fingers up at the world and plunge a whole fist into our pockets to keep life simple, convenient and 'more hygienic'. I would very much like to pretend that I fought the good fight and continue to happily scrub my child's nappies until my knuckles are raw. The truth is, I took the easy option and continue to buy disposable nappies to this day.

**Bloke's Rating:** Be realistic about how much effort is required and make your decision accordingly.

## Towel/Terry Nappies – Advanced

**Description:** Fortunately technology has advanced since the days when you were bundled up in your terry cloth. Enjoy the environmental and cash benefits of 'real' nappies with the new models – designed to resemble their disposable cousins, and just as straightforward to use. Nice.

**Pros:** With a plethora of groovy, Velcro-fastened numbers to choose from, shopping for nappies has never been so exciting! You will be able to choose nappies with printed patterns, or just keep it plain. Some have plastic covers, some not. Some come with disposable liners that you just flush down the loo with the poo. The manufacturers really are making it easier to be environmentally aware – it just boils down to whether you want to take the step or not.

**Cons:** Just as with the original Terries there is going to be more washing required and a regular interaction between your hand and your child's poo, but just think of all the money you'll save.

**What's it all about?** A strong argument for cloth nappies is that Baby can feel when he's wet/dirty, and he lets you know about it. That helps with potty training later on.

**Bloke's Rating:** If you've got the cash there are companies who wash the nappies for you and deliver them back smelling sweet as roses. Environmentally friendly and hassle-free. That's what we like.

## Nappy Sacks

**Description:** A nappy sack is a small plastic bag, usually fragranced, into which you can dispose of even the foulest-smelling disposable nappy. With a deft little knot the bag is sealed and you can reduce the smell of child poo pervading every corner of the house. If you are a dog owner then they're pretty handy for picking up their waste as well.

**Pros:** Beautiful as babies are, there's no escaping the fact that their poo stinks. The nappy sack will help. There are occasions when the mess created by a poo can result in you coming over all flushed and the only way to contain and control the mess is to use the best part of half a pack of wipes. Trying to deal with this bundle of messy nappy and skid-marked wipes is a feat in itself, holding a baby in your arms at the time just adds an extra challenge to the event – far easier to get everything bundled up into a nice little bag and into the bin as fast as possible.

**Cons:** Putting a disposable nappy into yet another layer of plastic will of course just add to the many decades it will take for your waste to degrade back into the earth. However, if you have made the decision to use disposable nappies, then it's a necessary evil.

**What's it all about?** As much as the fragrance works, I would still advise trying to get the nappy sack into an external bin as quickly as possible rather than having it fester for most of the day in your kitchen bin. Using nappy sacks is also good etiquette, especially when you find yourself cleaning your baby's bum in a public toilet or changing room.

**Bloke's Rating:** If you've decided on disposable nappies, then add nappy sacks to the shopping list.

## Nappy Bins

**Description:** A plastic bin with a special lid into which you can place a sodden and soiled nappy. A quick spin of the handle and the little pouch of foulness is contained in a scented bag and collected in the bin. Once full, the collection of nappies can be disposed of in your regular household waste receptacle – i.e. your wheelie bin.

**Pros:** When first attempting to change a newborn baby, the whole experience can be a nerve-racking, stressful, total body experience that ends up with Baby having a clean nappy, eventually, and you being covered in talc, cream, your child's poo and a selection of 'failed' nappies spread out over the floor. Panting and out of breath, you wipe your brow and then look down at the dirty nappy which has fallen poo-side down on the carpet or bed. You weep. This contraption won't fix any of the above problems, although you may have thought it would, but it does mean that you need not worry about carrying a dirty nappy as well as your newborn baby out of the room. The poo can stay, the child can travel – you feel much more comfortable holding Baby with both hands unencumbered.

**Cons:** The reality of changing nappies is that after you've done it twice it's really easy. In fact, you've become so cock-sure about it you've started timing yourself. Sixteen seconds is my personal best for a poo. Changing a child is not difficult and, therefore, you'll soon have no worries about carrying baby and a dirty nappy at the same time. The main downfall of the nappy bins is their capacity. While you can generate a string of sausage-like nappies all wrapped in a smell-vacuum, the bin can only handle about eight, so it's hardly worth the effort or the cost of rigging the plastic bags up.

**What's it all about?** In a bid for cleanliness and keeping Baby's world sanitary, not to mention our initial unfamiliarity with nappies and all they contain, it is not surprising that many couples choose to buy a nappy bin. I know we bought one. But don't. You'll only curse yourself in the future if you do.

**Bloke's Rating:** Don't be such a prude. Pick up the poo and remember to keep your fingernails short at all times.

## Wipes Warmer

**Description:** Baby has been asleep for the best part of two hours and is beginning to wake up. He's sleepy and slightly disorientated. Mum has been breastfeeding throughout the night and it's your turn to get up. Baby looks so peaceful sucking on his bottom lip and looking deep into your adoring eyes. You undo the poppers, take off the old nappy and apply a wipe – and then he starts to SCREAM, breathe, SCREAM, breathe. Now Mum is wide awake and wondering what's going on, Baby's crying and you're at a loss as to what went wrong. Cold wipes, that's what went wrong. How would you like it if someone placed a freezing cold wet flannel on your crown jewels a moment or two after you woke up? Actually, don't answer that. A wipes warmer is a small box into which you place your baby wipes. When you turn it on, it warms the wipes while keeping them moist. Simple, really.

**Pros:** No sudden temperature change, no upsetting screams in the middle of the night and just an all-round gentler way to clean Baby's bum. Other than the obvious, the science behind the warmer is that a warm wipe will open Baby's pores when you are cleaning and therefore be more effective than a cold wipe which causes the pores to close and therefore traps in bacteria. Mmm. Not really a problem if your child has a bath regularly.

**Cons:** Personally, I think the product is a rip-off, but I'll kindly keep my opinions to myself. If you want warm wipes, then the warmer will do the job. You will have to replace the special pillow which keeps the wipes moist inside the warmer every few months.

**What's it all about?** I've no doubt that these warmers are very popular and parents are buying them. I just don't get it. Tip: if you want to reduce the 'shock' of a cold wipe, be sure to wipe your child's knee or shin first; that way the initial wipe of the crotch is not so much of a surprise. Be warned that the application of a cold wipe onto any part of a baby's body can result in the rather spectacular and often unexpected surprise wee. Yes, he's been wearing the same nappy for four hours but only when his knee gets a bit chilled does he decide to let rip – all over you.

**Bloke's Rating**: Please! What's next, a nappy warmer?

## Changing Mat

**Description:** A length of plastic with foam-filled sides on which you can change your baby's nappy.

**Pros:** The plastic changing mat is a protective layer between the foulness that cometh forth from the pert little behind of your baby and your one-million-thread-count fine Egyptian cotton duvet cover. In a nutshell, it is far easier to wipe wee and poo from a changing mat than it is to remove it from bedcovers or the carpet. Changing mats are really cheap and come in a wide array of patterns with all of your favourite Disney or Pixar characters. The foam-filled sides help prevent a young baby from rolling around too much during the change.

**Cons:** Unless you perch the changing mat on top of a changing table or chest of drawers you will be forever bending over a bed, or kneeling on the floor every time you need to change the baby's nappy.

**What's it all about?** Maybe you're a dab hand at changing nappies, be they filled with wee or poo. Ninety-nine times out of a hundred you'll be a competent and effective bottom-cleaner. But, every now and again, and always when you least expect it, you'll be faced with the catastrophe of a filthy, *filthy* arse, so horrible, in fact, you just have to stand and stare for a minute wondering where on earth you are going to start. You know the situation I'm talking about – there's poo up her back and all round her bits; if you have a little lad then there's poo in the folds of his scrotum – it just makes you want to cry. And you will cry when you realise that the changing mat is tucked away in a cupboard on the other side of the room and you've already taken off the nappy. Yep, you've got poo on the bed and only your-self to blame. Those sheets were new on as well. Oh, what a fool you are.

**Bloke's Rating:** A life-saver and marriage-saver.

## Changing Table

**Description:** A two- or three-tier wooden platform on top of which you can change your baby's nappy. The other tiers are usually shelves for storing nappies, wipes, cream and talc etc.

**Pros:** The biggest plus to using a changing table is the height advantage over a changing mat. Of course, like sinks, they're never quite tall enough for blokes, but that's not an excuse not to use it. The onus is on you to speed up your nappy-changing technique before the pain in your lower back kicks in. Although some of the designs can look a little bit twee, there is something to be said for always having nappies and wipes to hand. There really is nothing worse than rushing to take off a nappy, only to find it is brimming with runny foulness so horrible you are gagging, and then to realise that you have left the wipes downstairs... What can you do? The answer: after much deliberation about leaving an infant unattended at the top of the stairs with a bare filthy arse, you do the right thing and cart him downstairs with that filthy arse rubbing itself all over your new shirt. Nice. Never again, not when you have all your wipes just a simple reach away!

**Cons:** There's not a lot that can be said against changing tables other than that the cheaper ones are a bit wobbly, and that will only get worse with general wear and tear, and then your baby getting bigger and heavier. I would advise paying a little bit extra and buying one that will last for this baby and the next.

**What's it all about?** Changing tables are nice but you'd be better-off buying a solid chest of drawers which will take up the same amount of space, and putting a changing mat on the top. Dedicate the top drawer to wipes and nappies and you've now got somewhere to put clothes, and a changing table in one. Clever, you see?

**Bloke's Rating:** Pretty, if you can afford it.

## Potty

**Description:** They can add as much extra plastic, shapes, bells and whistles as they like but a potty is a potty – a container for catching wee and poo when your toddler is starting to learn about life without nappies.

**Pros:** Whichever version you go for, using a potty is an essential stage of toilet training. Getting your child to use the potty rather than, say, the floor or the garden is a different matter, but I suppose that's part of the fun of fatherhood. Your child's first poo in a potty is a real milestone in her development and, although you won't be racing round to show the neighbours, you will smile and nod to yourself, acknowledging that your little girl is growing up.

**Cons:** Potties can be a little unstable and although your child may master the art of delivering waste into the potty, it only takes a swift kick or an attempt to pick up the full potty, for the contents to be sent flying across the floor. Some children are reluctant to use a potty because they don't see anyone else using one and therefore prefer to maintain the status quo – continue to wear nappies, or insist on trying to use the grown-up toilet. Potties also make great helmets and as long as they're empty that's funny, but you still need to nip that little game in the bud, otherwise your toddler is going to treat the potty as a toy, which it obviously isn't. Finally, your child's bladder and bowel control is not as finely tuned as yours and although for the majority of cases they will say they need their potty, there will be occasions when they just forget or get distracted. Be patient.

**What's it all about?** The toilet-training months can be frustrating for parents but a bit of empathy with your child is essential – your child has been wearing a nappy for her entire life, save bathtime. Now all of a sudden she's commando and that must take some getting used to. Kids don't see it as a huge problem when they mess their trousers – Mum or Dad is there to clean it all up. Eventually she'll get it right. Be sure to have numerous packets of wipes dotted throughout the house – poo time can be at any time and anywhere, so be prepared.

**Bloke's Rating:** An unpleasant but necessary step.

## Toilet Seat

**Description:** A child's toilet seat is a circle of plastic with a hole in the middle that is placed on top of your existing toilet seat, adding extra support and a smaller aperture so that your child doesn't fall through into the pan. Some toilet seats can be fixed on to your toilet in a semi-permanent way.

**Pros:** Some kids just want to bypass the whole potty experience and get straight onto the family throne. That's all very well, but ordinary toilet seats are a bit too big for little boys and girls, and this gadget takes potential minor injuries out of the equation. Toilet seats really instil a sense of independence compared to potties, although you will still be required to be on hand for wiping duties.

**Cons:** The cons are only really to Mum and especially to Dad if you go for the fixed toilet seat and there is only one toilet in the house – the extra seat can make it uncomfortable for Mum and Dad to sit on the toilet whilst having a piece of plastic wedged against their backs and you might have to hold the child's seat up by hand when you need a wee.

**What's it all about?** Using the toilet is something that we have to do every day; your child is no different. You will want to make the experience as quick and straightforward as you can.

**Bloke's Rating:** Many 'child toilet systems' contain both a potty and a toilet-seat element – this is by far the cheapest option and will give your kids a choice of pooing options.

## Foot Stool (for Toilets)

**Description:** It's all very well installing the child's toilet seat, but it's no good if the poor little mite can't reach the thing. A foot stool is what you need to give boys and girls that extra height so that they can climb onto the toilet, or for boys, take a wee standing up.

**Pros:** Leaving a foot stool in the bathroom means that you are going to be less and less involved with your child's excretions, which can only be a good thing.

**Cons:** Your child will now be able to reach things off shelves, and worktops, and to reach into cupboards, so you might have to reassess what gets stored where, now that they have access to a stool.

**What's it all about?** When buying a foot stool, be sure to buy a bathroom mat if you don't already have one. The foot stool can slide around and the mat will help keep it in one place.

**Bloke's Rating:** A necessary addition to your bathroom.

## Baby Bath

**Description:** A plastic tub in which you bathe your baby. Incredibly simple, incredibly cheap, but you'll need to be bench-pressing 400lbs before you can pick up a full one without a) spilling water or b) straining your back. Most parents learn how heavy and unstable a few gallons of water can be after just one attempt. Anyone who has a fish tank learned the lesson long ago – but we've all caught up now.

**Pros:** Plastic baby baths offer the chance to bathe your baby in relative ease. Once the bath is filled with warm water, just add Baby. Unlike your household bath, the sides aren't annoyingly high to lean over when you're trying to keep hold of your baby in the water. There is also a very simple ecological argument for baby baths – they use less water to fill than an ordinary tub.

**Cons:** Other than trying to lift a full one, there isn't really anything bad about baby baths.

**What's it all about?** Bring the baby to the bath, not the other way round. Best to fill it in the bathroom so that you can get rid of the dirty water easily and any spillages can be contained.

**Bloke's Rating:** It's one of those purchases that you feel you simply must have when your partner is expecting. For us, and for most of our friends, the baby bath was used for a couple of weeks only and then baby was in the regular bath with Mum or Dad. It's a confidence issue and when you are just getting to grips with handling a newborn, you want control of the situation and suddenly the sides of the house bath seem too high and too scary. A few weeks pass and you're quite the dab hand at handling your baby.

## Baby Bath (Bucket)

**Description:** This really is just a large bucket into which you put water and a baby. The design is based on the idea that babies really liked it in the womb and that by bathing your child in one of these contraptions, they will feel comfortable, secure and safe and you get a clean child at the end of it.

**Pros:** The design means that very young babies have the support they need to stay upright in the bath. You dictate how much water to add, and again, because your baby is slotted into the gap, there isn't the chance of baby slipping or her head going under the water as there is with a baby bath or regular bath. There is something incredibly cute about a bucket-o-baby and it is quite staggering just how comfortable and how natural sitting in the foetal position is for newborns.

**Cons:** As with the regular run-of-the-mill baby bath, you are not going to want to cart this thing around the house when it's full – that will really hurt. There's obviously a limited lifespan with bucket baths as your baby grows, but this is true of all baby baths. I feel that the baby bucket might offer a lot more in terms of safety, but the compromise is your baby's ability to move around in a bath freely, to splash and to play with toys.

**What's it all about?** Bucket baths or Tummy Tubs are a recent import from continental Europe and are only just beginning to take hold in the UK. I think they will replace the baby bath as the preferred choice for washing kids who are under about four months.

**Bloke's Rating:** Given the choice between a standard baby bath and a baby bucket, go for the bucket.

## Bath Toys – Large

**Description:** There's nothing more desolate than a large bath. Although you might fill the bath quite comfortably, babies and toddlers are usually dwarfed by the imposing fibreglass expanse. Brighten up their lives with one or two large bath toys. The most common of these are water-wheels, available in a vast array of complexities, or Baby's own armada of boats.

**Pros:** Items such as boats or waterwheels really do make bath time a lot of fun. In the early days you are more concerned with pragmatically cleaning your child, but once they are able to sit, bath time becomes another activity in Baby's busy day. Encouraging your child's enjoyment of water has many long-term benefits which will become evident when they start to learn to swim.

**Cons:** All of these bath-specific toys need to be stored

somewhere when it's not actually bath time. For many of us, that means in the bath itself, because there's simply nowhere else. Great for Baby, but it means transferring everything on to the bathroom floor when you or your partner wants to bathe or shower – and then transferring it all back again when you have finished. Kind of puts an end to the idea of a quick shower for the next few years.

**What's it all about?** In terms of creating routines for your child, it is important to look at bath time as another valuable period of the day. For most of us it immediately precedes bedtime and some would argue that this is about chilling out and calming down after a hard day's play. But messing about in the bath can be stimulating while remaining reasonably calm.

**Bloke's Rating:** Waterwheels are brilliant. When you've finished playing with it yourself, let your baby have a go or there'll be tears before bedtime.

## Bath Toys – Small

**Description:** Sometimes the large bath toys by themselves just don't cut the mustard. As with the toy box in the sitting room, you also need to have a bit of a collection in the bathroom. This could be a selection of the ubiquitous yellow plastic ducks, or it could be one of the many 'squirty' toys available on the market.

**Pros:** Squirty toys often squeak when squeezed. They seem to amuse babies and toddlers no end, except when the water in the toy has been there since yesterday's bath and is therefore freezing cold. Squeeze that playfully at their belly and they don't like it. They don't like that at all!

We found that that as our children got older we could ask them to fetch the yellow boat or the orange fish, and before long they had mastered colours, or at least the five different colours represented by bath toys – so there you have it: not only are bath toys fun, but they're also educational! Sometimes the simplest of items can become toys. Our son loves playing with a plastic takeaway carton, which he uses to pour water onto the waterwheel or over his sister's head. You don't have to blow the budget on bath toys, just use what you have in the house.

**Cons:** Over the course of the coming years the floor of your bathroom is going to get soaked and there's not a tremendous amount that you can do about it. Most of this is down to the inordinate amount of splashing that occurs at bath time, but added to that problem is the amount of water that is bailed out of the bath, on to the floor, by containers you provide for your children to play with...

You should also think about where you store your toys, especially if they are still wet. A wooden box will eventually grow mould and begin to rot. A metal container will begin to rust. A plastic box is what you need.

**What's it all about?** A bit of spilt water never hurts anyone. Chill out and let your baby have fun. Also expect the hilarious game of toys being thrown out of the bath and your job as chief retrieval officer. They like that, those pesky kids.

**Bloke's Rating:** Splish, splash – let's give the kids a bath.

## Bath Toy Organiser

**Description:** A storage facility for bath toys allowing your bathroom to stay reasonably neat and tidy throughout the day. You need one for all of your remote controls and you'll need one for all of the bath toys you've got. Organisers can be plastic contraptions or simple fabric bags that fit to the side of the bath.

**Pros:** If you've gone to the trouble of buying toys for your child, you might as well complete the picture with somewhere suitable to store them. Having a bath toy organiser means that the toys are close to hand when you need them and not under your feet when you need a bath or a shower. Allowing the wet toys to hang over the bath allows for safe drip-drying, rather than creating new cultures in the boiler cupboard or in the soap dish.

**Cons:** None.

**What's it all about?** Having the ability to store and generally tidy up at the end of your child's day is one of the few blessings left to the tired Mum or Dad who has been looking after the little one all day. It can sometimes feel like a losing battle to try to enjoy an hour or two of peace, quiet and cleanliness in the interval between Baby's bedtime and your own attempt to get to sleep – ready for it all to begin again in the morning. Being able to neatly store the baby's bath toys may just be a minor point, but being able to take a shower or a bath without standing or slipping on a purple rubber octopus is a major victory at the end of a tiring day of childcare.

**Bloke's Rating:** Tidy up the toys!

## Hooded Baby Towel / Poncho for Beach

**Description:** It's a towel with a bit folded over to form a hood. Simple really, but sometimes simplicity is best. These incredibly soft towels are big enough to wrap around a baby and the handy hood keeps their head warm after you've washed their hair.

**Pros:** As I said earlier we all lose 70% of our body heat through our head, so if you've just washed your baby's head, you're going to want to wrap it up. A hooded baby towel does just that.

**Cons:** None, apart from the baby towels with the silly ears sticking out or with eyes printed on them. Far too silly.

**What's it all about?** Obviously an ordinary bath towel will do the trick. Baby will be dry in a matter of seconds and he won't feel like he missed out on a must-have fashion accessory thus leading to a complex in later years. However, for sheer 'cute factor', buy a hooded baby towel.

**Bloke's Rating:** Photo opportunity.

## Bath/Shower Mat

**Description:** Chances are you will have a bath/shower mat already, but if you don't, you simply must buy one. Babies are very wriggly and the phrase 'slippery when wet' is never truer than when referring to a baby in a bath. Once your baby starts trying to move around in the bath, no matter how shallow the water, you will want to employ every technique available to keep bath time fun and stop it turning into an extreme sport. A bath mat helps.

**Pros:** Cheap. Safe.

**Cons:** So it might spoil the beautiful lines and detract

from the very expensive taps and shower head that you've just had fitted, but you'll already have noticed the theme here – having kids wrecks the aesthetics of your home. Get over it.

**What's it all about?** A plastic or rubber mat can be the thing that saves you or your baby from taking a nasty tumble. You can always hide it in a cupboard and bring it out for bath time, along with the box full of plastic ducks, the water-wheel, the glove-puppet flannels and the wide array of baby bathing products. Or you can hold your head up high and leave it all out on display – every other room looks like a tip, why not the bathroom?

**Bloke's Rating:** An essential requirement.

## Bath Ring/Seat

**Description:** Your baby will be a year old before he starts to get the hang of balancing. Even if your baby is sitting and can sit for a good half an hour, it only takes one slip. That's not an option at bathtime. Squirminess is always a factor too – especially if you are trying to bathe your child in a full-size adult bath. The answer could be a bath ring. A bath ring is a plastic seat that contains your baby, keeping him upright in the bath and more importantly keeping baby's head away from the water. Most bath rings come with plastic or rubber suckers that fix the ring firmly in position on the bottom of the tub.

**Pros:** The seat does allow enough room for your baby to move around a bit and play, similar, in fact, to the movement they have in a high chair. A bath ring is reasonably cheap and may well give you extra confidence at bath time. Most bath rings include a few activities on the 'dashboard' for babies to fiddle with when they're in the bath.

**Cons:** Most families get away without using a bath ring. In my opinion, during the early months you should look at bath time from a practical point of view only – an opportunity to wash your baby. Although play should be encouraged, this can all be managed in a matter of minutes. Once your child is about a year old they will be far more confident in the water and you'll be able to take a much more back-seat role, allowing them the full length and breadth of the bath in which to explore, play and splash – of course, you should never leave the room with a child in the bath, no matter how confident they appear. Just let the phone ring and call whoever it is back later.

**What's it all about?** More clutter in the bathroom, to be honest. The obvious alternatives are to a) get in the bath as well, but this isn't always possible, b) resign yourself to holding your baby throughout bath time, or c) not wash your child.

## Baby Grooming Products

**Description:** Although you can quite easily get away with using the items you've already got lying around the house, you might find that when you first try to cut your baby's nails with the enormous toenail clippers you'll panic and worry that you might in fact cut off the whole toe in one fell swoop. That's why there are baby grooming products for sale – nail clippers, scissors, comb, hairbrush, tweezers. You'll need them all.

**Pros:** Thankfully Baby's nails don't grow as fast as yours and the nails themselves are far flimsier than on an adult, but grow they do, and you wouldn't want your baby to accidentally catch one and pull the nail off. So, every six weeks or so, just after their bath comes the intricate experience of cutting nails, which requires two adults on hand. The miniature nail clippers are just the ticket. The tweezers are really useful when certain things are jammed up noses – expect to be retrieving bits of tissue, plastic, Play Dough and mud.

**Cons:** Yes, it's just more stuff to lose, but that's no reason not to buy it.

**What's it all about?** It doesn't feel right trying to brush through their hair with your manky old dandruff-covered comb – their hair deserves better!

**Bloke's Rating:** Keep Baby's kit in its own pouch or container, otherwise it won't last a week.

# Mess Tent

Eating and drinking are a major element to our lives. Most of us eat three times a day and spend plenty of time buying, preparing and cooking food – add on the time it takes to eat it and then the tidying and washing-up, and the hours really pile up. Now you have a baby, this entire process is multiplied. Everything takes longer, from the thorough washing of vegetables to the cleaning of the high chair. Just as the last pot is put away in the cupboard it's time to get the next meal under way and start the whole process all over again.

You'll want to invest in most of the gadgets available to make your life far easier and for you to be able to get as much food as possible into your baby's mouth with the minimum fuss and the minimum mess. Everything from having a bigger fridge to buying special baby cutlery will help. These are the gadgets that are going to make the difference.

## Baby Bottles

**Description:** Plastic bottles of varying capacity with a rubber nipple or teat from which Baby can drink liquids.

**Pros:** Baby's mouth and tongue are pre-programmed to suckle from Mum's breast. There's no point presenting Baby with a pint glass full of milk and expecting him to know what on earth he's supposed to do with it. A baby bottle is shaped to make it easy for Mum, Dad or Baby to grip, and the rubber teat mimics the nipple, making it reasonably straightforward for Baby to work out what's going on and to be feeding in no time at all. If you have a steriliser, the baby bottles are easy to clean and if you buy a few, you can have natural or formula milk ready-prepared in the fridge for easy access.

**Cons:** None, although once Baby has a few teeth the rubber teats can become quite chewed. By this stage you will be wanting to move on to trainer cups.

**What's it all about?** Whether you are planning to feed with expressed or formula milk or neither, it is certainly worth having a bottle or two in the house, for no better reason than they're great if you need to give your baby a drink of water, say if you go abroad on holiday, or even when we occasionally enjoy a very hot day here in the UK.

**Bloke's Rating:** Have a go at drinking water or juice from a bottle yourself. It's strangely pleasant and exciting – or maybe that's just me.

## Bottle Cleaners

**Description:** Incredibly small and fine plastic or wire brushes used specifically for cleaning bottle teats or the mouth-piece of a training cup. Not dissimilar to a mini-toothbrush, these little gadgets help remove any microscopic bits of leftover milk or nasty germs.

**Pros:** Brushes are reasonably cheap and easily available. If you have bought a steriliser it's more than likely that the manufacturer will have thrown a few of these brushes in with the set. Cleaning bottles and cups won't, of course, stop your child from ever getting ill, but it will go a long way to minimising avoidable illness.

**Cons:** Don't forget to wash the brush itself regularly, otherwise you will just be transferring the same germs back and forth. A regular scalding – bad brush, naughty brush – in boiling water or a quick turn in the dishwasher should do the trick. When you are choosing your brushes don't just buy the first pack you see. Shop around. Blokes are generally blessed with ham-like fists, which are fab when you are needed to open stubborn jars or carry sofas in or out of a house, but a curse when it comes to trying to squeeze your fingers into the very narrow confines of a baby bottle. Buy brushes with long handles.

**What's it all about?** Sadly, for the lazy washer-upper – something us blokes get accused of being – washing your baby's bottle or trainer cup in warm soapy water isn't enough. You need to be scrubbing every last bit and paying particular attention to the areas that are in constant air and mouth contact. Leftover milk goes off and within a matter of hours becomes a hotbed of germs for your baby to ingest during his next feed. The result can be two or three days of sickness and/or diarrhoea, which, I'm sure you are aware, is far from pleasant. An extra two minutes of scouring can prevent it.

**Bloke's Rating:** Simple and effective – get scrubbing.

## Sterilisers

**Description:** Sterilisers are either stand-alone products, which you plug into a socket, or else they are designed for use in a microwave. Either way, the principle is to steam the baby bottles and teats at such a high temperature, and for so long, that any nasty germs or bacteria are completely nuked.

**Pros:** Without a doubt a steriliser will do a far more thorough job of cleaning your baby's bottle and teats than you can manage in the washing-up bowl. That said, you are still expected to wash the bottles and teats in warm soapy water, but the steriliser is all about *getting rid of the dirt you can see and the germs you can't*. Milk, both natural and formula, goes off very quickly and those tiny fiddly bits of rubber and plastic are ideal breeding grounds for all sorts of horrible sickness-causing bacteria, even if you've scoured off any particles visible to the naked eye.

**Cons:** When the steriliser has finished its cycle, don't rush in and start grabbing bottles and teats – those things remain painfully hot for a good ten or twenty minutes.

**What's it all about?** If you are planning to use formula milk or your partner is planning to express milk, then you are going to need to buy a steriliser. The microwave sterilisers are about half the price of the stand-alone versions, but you can probably get double the stuff into the latter.

**Bloke's Rating:** A lot of money for steam, but it works.

## High Chair

**Description:** The high chair will be one of your 'big' essentials when your partner is expecting, or shortly after your first child is born. Obviously, if you can get one from a friend for free, go for it. If not, try tapping the doting grandparents for one. Thirdly, if all else fails, then you'll have to buy one. Damn... High chairs come in a range of sizes and are generally made out of wood or plastic. The basic idea is to raise the child up to table height and to keep them secure. High chairs can either be pulled up to the kitchen table so that Baby can sit with the grown-ups and steal toast from your plate, or else the chair can come with its own independent table.

**Pros:** A high chair with its own table works for many children because they can see what's going on with everyone else in the family, while at the same time remaining far enough removed to concentrate on eating their own food. By placing your child in a high chair it is a sure sign that it is now time to eat. Over a period of a few weeks this connection will be learned and your child will lay down his toys and understand that it's time to enjoy a bowl of beans and not play – although this is not always the case. A high chair is useful when you want to get your baby, or toddler, to calm down – the sudden change of perspective and the raised vista alter your baby's environment so suddenly that they often forget what it was they were upset about. Some parents insist on using the high chair for snacks as well as main meals to ensure that eating is done sitting down and not while running round the house.

**Cons:** Bringing very young children to the table can feel fair and right, but often the stimulation – especially if there are other, older children in the house – can be too much – resulting in dinner left uneaten or thrown on the floor. One unavoidable downfall with the plastic-covered high chairs is the amount of muck that gets caught up in the folds and the creases of the material and on the straps. No matter how clean an eater your baby is, no matter how well you mop up after every meal, when it comes to cleaning the high chair, you will find all sorts of horrors that will make you wish you could feed your baby intravenously.

**What's it all about?** High chairs are a totally necessary addition to the kitchen/dining room. They're big, clumsy and not particularly attractive, but they really do work. Although it is very funny and cute to have your toddler or baby poke their head up from a grown-up's seat, they're not really going to eat an awful lot of food when they're the centre of attention and when it's so easy to escape from the table. As cruel as it may seem, you need to pen them in and treat them like the age they are – one – which means strapping them in and getting very cross when they don't eat the full portion of broccoli.

**Bloke's Rating:** High chairs are solid, but if you come across ones that proclaim they'll last for ten or more years, the makers are lying to you. Lying through their teeth, in fact. No child is that passive and no chair is that hard. There's a lifespan, and once that lifespan is reached, it all collapses into a plastic and wooden mess on the floor.

## High Chair Toys

**Description:** There is a large range of toys available for babies in high chairs. As a parent you can choose to ignore or embrace the selection. Generally the toys available are simple devices that encourage your child to hit, tap or spin a piece of plastic. The toy itself is either fixed on with a pressure bolt or secured with a suction cup to the table of your child's high chair. The toys are generally bright and fun and some offer the added advantage of a squeak, which is great for the baby, but quite annoying for you.

**Pros:** Eating with a toddler is fine, if there is only one course of food. However, the moment you introduce either a starter or a dessert, or, heaven forbid, *both*, into the equation, suddenly it's going to be a long time for Baby to tolerate sitting still in a high chair. That's where the toys come into play. Sometimes there are periods of time between courses that can easily be passed by the adults through the art of conversation – how jolly to be so old and wise. For kids, this 'nothing time' is utter pants and you can call it what you want, but it does not detract from the fact that they are stuck in a high chair with a piece of raw carrot and some hummus, while you're half-cut on Stella Artois and a cheap bottle of red because you've got nothing more substantial in your stomach than a rather poor prawn cocktail... If you're eating out, order the kid's meal to come out with your starter, otherwise you might as well not bother going out to eat.

**Cons:** If you're embarrassed about pulling out a couple of toy trains, a Mr Incredible and a My Little Pony from your bag in a busy restaurant, then you're probably not parenting material. High chair toys, just like all the other toys you have bought, will be thrown across the room and thrown at your head. It's how these things work. Get over it.

**What's it all about?** More clutter, yes. But just like you have specific toys that only come out at bath time, it's equally important to have certain toys that make an appearance only at dinner time. This is not to say that a child who is not eating his greens is rewarded with playtime, but more that you can introduce a bit of fun into meal times and ensure that your child is eating a nice, healthy, balanced diet.

**Bloke's Rating:** Toys rule, you know that and your baby knows that. Don't wait for my opinion, get buying.

## Electric Blender

**Description:** These mixers are hand-held devices for blending soft foodstuffs and turning them into soup or purée. If you can stand the sound it makes, they're also pretty useful for crushing ice, which can be used in exotic cocktails or just to make your own slush.

**Pros:** Young babies need to be fed liquid food when they are first weaning – you can obviously take the easy option and buy it in overpriced jars from the supermarket, or you can start experimenting with sweet potatoes, butternut squash and turnip. You'll be surprised at the sloppy concoctions you'll be able to create. At the time of writing, Tesco were selling blenders for less than £5 – there's really no excuse.

**Cons:** Mixers often come with a plastic measuring cup. Never add boiling water or soup to a measuring cup direct. They tend to crack and you get a stream of boiling liquid over your groin – painful and hard to explain away.

**What's it all about?** Every home should really have one already, but if you don't, buy one. Useful for soups too. Mush up your own meals for Baby. They're cheaper and probably a lot healthier for him – assuming you don't eat kebabs every night.

**Bloke's Rating:** A kitchen must.

## Baby Cutlery

**Description:** Knives, forks and spoons designed especially for babies and toddlers. Some baby cutlery just consists of miniature versions of regular knives and forks and some are specially designed and shaped for Baby's tiny fingers to wrap around.

**Pros:** When you first see your baby grab an adult knife and fork you will panic at how lethal and dangerous simple household cutlery can look in the hands of an infant. All that waving of metal in the air is too much – especially when they start waving the fork a bit too close to their nose or eye. Baby cutlery has far more plastic than normal cutlery, and any knives or forks made with metal bits are considerably smaller and more blunt than their adult companions.

**Cons:** None.

**What's it all about?** Believe it or not, there will come a time when you don't have to scoop every single mouthful of food from bowl to mouth. There comes a time when Baby wants to be an independent eater, and although this will mainly be achieved by trying to pick soup up with her fingers, she will want to give the spoon a go too – play fair and give her a chance.

**Bloke's Rating:** Most ergonomic cutlery looks a bit like it has been left too near a hot oven and it has melted –

although it looks daft, so does your baby trying to use grown-up cutlery. These strange pieces of plastic really work and mean that Baby can start to feed himself sooner, and with far more accuracy.

## Bibs

**Description:** A square of plastic or cotton that you place around the neck of your child to minimise the amount of spilt food, saliva and vomit that lands on their clothes. Most young babies will need to wear cloth bibs continuously for the first few months to catch all that dribble and puke.

**Pros:** The advantage of the plastic bib is the trough at the bottom for catching bits. Not much use if your baby is eating yoghurt, but great if there's something a bit more solid. Babies tend to fish food out of the trough and continue munching, allowing you a welcome minute or so to eat your own dinner, which is now stone-cold.

**Cons:** Bibs can give you a false sense of security. They won't catch everything, or stop spillages. Although your baby's jumper might remain perfect, his trousers are likely to need replacing after every meal. Some babies will not like wearing a bib and will spend more time trying to take the thing off than eating their food, which sort-of defeats the purpose. Once it gets to this stage you are fighting a losing battle. When tossed across the kitchen, a plastic bib containing all manner of horrors makes a right old mess. Stop trying to put one on the child at this point.

**What's it all about?** Feeding a baby can become quite stressful, especially when they try to assert their independence and try to help... Do yourself a favour and have a huge stockpile of bibs that can be tossed into the sink or the washing machine after each meal.

**Bloke's Rating:** Bibs are great.

## Trainer Cup

**Description:** A plastic cup with an airtight removable lid and two handles for baby to clasp. The lid keeps the drink in and grubby fingers and foreign bodies out. This is the way forward for babies once they move on from the breast or the bottle and before they are ready to attack a pint of snakebite. Baby cups come in a wide array of shapes and colours but they're all pretty much the same. Most trainer cups are fitted with a non-drip valve; ensure yours is.

**Pros:** Babies throw their cups around the room all the time. They will throw their cup from their high chair, their pram and when they're standing in the middle of the room – without provocation and with extreme prejudice. Without a lid you'd be forever cleaning up spills and wiping down walls – not to mention changing your clothes.

The non-drip valve and the sealed lid are exactly what you want to stop excessive spills and accidents. Once your baby is using a trainer cup it really marks a new phase in their development. They can help themselves when they are thirsty and some of the pressure to be breastfeeding non-stop all day will be off Mum.

**Cons:** Some of the lids are so effective it is actually quite difficult to get the thing off when you need to. If there's a bit of drink left in the bottom of the cup, then you won't be the first or the last dad to have spilt it, meaning that you've actually made more mess than the baby. With some training cups the valve can come loose from the mouthpiece, which abruptly ends its non-drip appeal. It is also worth buying two cups exactly the same for when you or the baby loses one.

**What's it all about?** Some parents worry that their child will become too attached to a baby cup and will still want to use them when they're five years old and going to school. This is highly unlikely. Your responsibility is to ensure your baby drinks enough fluids during the day. Your baby or toddler will want to drink out of a proper cup or glass just like Daddy, but it's a skill that is going to take some practice. In the meantime a trainer cup will provide them with their liquid refreshment and protect your carpets from lashings and lashings of sticky juice.

**Bloke's Rating:** Useful. Dirt cheap, highly effective. Thumbs up.

## Eating/Painting Suits

**Description:** Waterproof plastic clothing worn over your child's regular clothes to prevent any nasty stains or having to change them three times a day. Some suits include trousers, but most are smocks, which are either worn like jackets, with a zip or ties at the front or the back, or, like jumpers, pulled over the head.

**Pros:** The transition period when your child no longer wants to be fed like a baby, but hasn't quite mastered the art of holding a spoon without spilling the contents on himself, is a frustrating one for parents and toddlers. You don't mind too much if they make a mess with their evening meal – they'll be going in the bath soon anyway. It's when they have yoghurt all over their clothes by ten o'clock in the morning that you need to be using an eating suit.

**Cons:** The jumper-like smocks are great until it comes to taking one off when it's covered in spilt food. This can lead to more mess than if you hadn't bothered in the first place.

**What's it all about?** It may seem somewhat extreme, but then feeding time can be appallingly messy. If it makes you feel better, be sure to have an art activity planned immediately after dinner time, and tell yourself that you just decided to change your child in anticipation.

**Bloke's Rating:** When your baby gets to the stage of being able to pull off their bib, you'll want to invest in an eating suit.

## Jar Opener Gadget

**Description:** An easy way to open stubborn jars of baby food. Clamp the grippers around the lid of your chosen jar and, with a little squeeze and a turn, the lid comes off.

**Pros:** With minimum effort and ladylike wrists you can open the most stubborn of jars.

**Cons:** Any man with self-respect will avoid this, unless no one is looking.

**What's it all about?** It basically breaks the air seal between a jar and a lid, thus allowing easier twist-off capabilities. Makes you look dead hard. Assuming no one sees you using it. I have an excuse – I broke my wrist, twice. Maybe you did too, or maybe you're a big girl's blouse? No matter, either way, sometimes opening a stubborn jar of food is tantamount to removing the sword from the stone. It hurts if you get it wrong and you look and feel like the daddy-don if you get it right. But you have another option, and that option is cheating. The jar opener gadget will assist in all those weak-wristed moments. Buy one; keep it in the drawer with the kebab skewers, just in case. No jar is tougher than you.

**Bloke's Rating:** Keep it secret, keep it safe.

## Frozen Orange Cartons

**Description:** Freeze a couple of single-serving orange juice cartons to act as ideal cool-bag coolers

**Pros:** Cartons of orange juice cost next to nothing. The foil-lined packaging will last for years longer than ice packs, and they don't leak. Every time you want to keep stuff fresh, you will know that there are two or more frozen orange packs to hand in the freezer.

**Cons:** If you're particularly bothered about how things look, then yes, using frozen orange juice cartons to keep your sandwiches fresh is pretty cheap, but surely the mug is the person who spent money buying ice... and now has soggy sandwiches. And that's not you. Your frozen orange juice may well defrost over the course of one day, but the beauty is, assuming that you never intend to drink the contents, you can simply freeze it again. It will last forever. Permafrost for less than a pound. It's got my vote.

**What's it all about?** Be practical, be realistic. It's important to keep things inexpensive. Look for alternatives where you can. Life is pricey enough without giving in to the marketing ethic. Use and re-use frozen orange juice again and again.

**Bloke's Rating:** Cheap and cheerful.

## Suction Cup Food Bowl

**Description:** The ideal way to keep Baby's food in one place as you practise the often-trying art of feeding a restless toddler.

**Pros:** Theoretically, no matter how much your industrious child wants to move around, his or her food will stay still in the suction cup bowl. Secure, safe and static. That's what you want and what one would expect from a suction cup system. Is that what you get? Is it, bollocks...

**Cons:** The reality is that the suction just isn't 'sucky' enough. The suction cup may stick the bowl to the tray or the table, but the planners behind this concept basically ignored the baby factor. My seventeen-month-old son, for example, can pick up about three times his own body weight and throw it – accurately – against anything that resembles my head, and that usually transpires to be my head. When faced with a bowl that was 'stuck' to his high chair he made a concerted effort to remove said bowl and, as if he was challenging the technicians, succeeded and threw it at my head. Again. It really hurt. Suckers or not, it was not a static bowl. Opt for a soft-plastic feeding bowl that allows food to cool quickly, doesn't break on impact with the floor or your face, and is big enough to excite your child on presentation. The more excited they are about receiving their dinner, the less likely they are to throw it all in your face.

**Bloke's Rating:** Never mind the suckers!

# Big Fridge/Freezer

**Description:** A big fridge is like a little fridge, only bigger. An electrical storage device to keep food and drinks cool and fresh. A freezer is similar, only everything is kept at sub-zero temperatures. But you probably knew all that already. They usually come in white, silver or black.

**Pros:** Obviously no modern home is complete without a fridge, but a big fridge will simply allow you to store more items. A box freezer is fine to keep ice, but little else. It's time to expand and up the capacity. Whoever is staying home with the baby is going to be cooking in bulk and then freezing lots of mini-portions of baby food. Having to pick away at the ice in the broken freezer box just isn't tennis.

**Cons:** A big fridge will take up room in your kitchen or any other room, but it really is a necessity. There's obviously an ecological argument against the added power consumption of a large fridge-freezer but we'll have that argument after you get rid of your car, gas central heating, television and when you stop flying abroad. Having a baby is not about minimalism, I'm afraid. Put your hand in your pocket and shop.

**What's it all about?** No matter how large the fridge you have at the moment, chances are you are going to need a bigger one. There are hundreds on the market. Don't be waylaid with the ones with fancy computers telling you that your milk will run out in 2.5 hours and your broccoli needs to be used up by Friday of last week. You need to concentrate on storage capacity. Buy as big as your home will allow. The amount of pulped vegetables and pre-made baby dinners that are going to be fighting for space in your fridge and freezer is absolutely shocking. You'll be lucky to be able to keep the mayonnaise cool, never mind your four-pack of beer.

**Bloke's Rating:** Cool.

# Dishwasher

**Description:** Automated washing device for all your dirty crockery, cutlery, pots and pans.

**Pros:** When there were just the two of you, life offered so many spare moments during the day, even if you were both working full time. The washing-up was a quick five- or ten-minute activity that the two of you could share before sitting down to *Millionaire* and a drop of red wine – and then Baby came along. Never, or not for at least another eighteen years, will you ever get a spare moment, or for that matter be able to do the washing-up in just five minutes. A dishwasher will become your trusty friend, taking care of the majority of your dirty dishes, leaving you more time to do all the other things that need to be done around the house.

**Cons:** None, apart from the environmental damage of detergents, but as you already use a washing machine, we'll just ignore that, shall we?

**What's it all about?** A dishwasher was once seen as a luxury or a nice extra. When you have kids, it's a necessity. If you really haven't got the space for a standard-size dishwasher, don't forget you can get smaller counter-mounted versions that might just be the ticket.

**Bloke's Rating:** For truly Fairy soft hands, buy one of these.

# Deployment Overseas

You will be very pleased to learn that having kids does not stop the young mum and dad, or even the older mum and dad, from taking themselves off for a short break – be it somewhere new in Britain or somewhere further afield. Oh, yes. You can go on holiday with kids, no problem. The only difference of course, compared to the halcyon days of yester-year, is that a holiday no longer means a week of lying prone on a hot beach with a book over your face. In fact, a holiday with kids is really hard work and you won't be the first parents to wish on occasion that you'd stayed at home.

On the flip side, your kids will enjoy time away from the house so much that you'll willingly go through the misery and hard work of holidays again and again just for their pleasure, with absolutely no concern for your own or your partner's enjoyment. There is something so profoundly satisfying about taking kids to a beach, or a campsite, or staying in a hotel, or a hired cottage. It's so magical for them that it actually ends up being infectious. To you, your accommodation may look shoddy, tired and generally disappointing – does your toddler give a damn about the poor quality of grouting in the bathroom? Does he, bollocks. There are other kids to play with, an enormous beach to explore and he's allowed to stay up an hour or two later than normal – this is toddler heaven.

By now you won't be surprised to learn that manu-facturers have cottoned on to the fact that even parents need a vacation every now and again, and yes, they've produced a whole arsenal of gadgets to make Baby's holiday experience even more magical. Dig deep, you're off on your hols.

## Travel Cot

**Description:** It doesn't take much to define a travel cot, but it would take a long time to discuss the clever way in which the engineer came up with the ingenious design for the collapsible arms. The collapsible arms are fantastic when you are erecting the travel cot, but come the next morning when the hotel is demanding that you check out, or when you've only got half an hour to get to the airport, can you collapse the thing down? Nope. After some brute force and some choice language the travel cot will once again travel, but not before you have erected it again countless times and tried collapsing each individual arm in rotating order. Finally, you get it right.

**Pros:** Travel cots open up a whole gamut of possibilities for getting out and about. Having a travel cot in the house is also super when friends come to visit who are also in the family way. Travel cots are flimsier than their big wooden counterparts, but because they're floor-based rather than standing on legs, there's no escape for the little one.

**Cons:** Other than the whole putting-the-thing-back-in-its-bag fiasco, there's not a lot wrong with travel cots. On first appraisal the mattress in the travel cot can seem to be a bit stiff and not particularly welcoming for your little baby, but it doesn't seem to bother them at all. To be honest, our son uses his as his permanent cot.

**What's it all about?** Having a baby does impact your ability to go out for a nice meal or even catch a movie in the cinema, but it shouldn't impede going on holiday or visiting friends and family. With a travel cot you're mobile again.

**Bloke's Rating:** The second most important gadget you can buy.

## Swimming Nappies

**Description:** Swimming nappies are nappies that won't disintegrate in water but will still catch any surprise accidents when you're at the pool or on the beach. As with regular nappies, you can choose between disposable and re-usable swim nappies. If you decide on the re-usable, then go for the drawstring variation rather than the pants style – the drawstring nappies are far easier to remove when there's been a poo incident without it turning into a horrible, horrible mess.

**Pros:** If you're planning to take your baby swimming or paddling, then you are going to need swimming nappies to be able to use a public pool. You can probably get away with letting him run around starkers at the beach, but it would be polite to put a nappy on anyway, as the chances are his bowel will open on someone's towel.

**Cons:** None.

**What's it all about?** Worth buying a re-usable swimming nappy even if you ordinarily use disposables – you won't be going swimming that often, so it's unlikely you'll have to clean too many poos. The disposable swimming nappies are really expensive.

**Bloke's Rating:** Get your kids into swimming as soon as you can.

## Swimming/Water Shoes

**Description:** Rubber or plastic shoes to protect little feet from stones and hot sand. Water shoes also provide grip when there is a lot of spilt water at the side of a pool. Kids can go in and out of the water wearing their water shoes and not worry about having their toes nipped by crabs when exploring rock pools.

**Pros:** It may be too cold to go swimming, but that doesn't mean that splashing her feet is out of the question. Keeping these shoes in the car is great in case you suddenly find a stream to explore. They will also protect against sunburn.

**Cons:** The rubber versions especially can be a bugger to get on and off; a trick is make both the shoes and your child's feet wet before trying to put them on and to try and take the shoes off in water, if that's possible.

**What's it all about?** Playing on the beach can be loads of fun, but if you find yourself on holiday and you pop down to the beach, there can sometimes be a couple of hundred yards of foot-melting sand to traverse before you get to the water. You don't want to get her only pair of shoes full of sand and you can't let her walk barefoot. Water shoes. That's what you need.

**Bloke's Rating:** Surf's up.

## Baby Flotation Vest

**Description:** Baby flotation vests usually look like life jackets and work in much the same way. Rather than being inflated by air, these jackets have blocks of foam inserted in purpose-built pockets to offer your baby a more independent swim, while still keeping her safe and holding her head out of the water.

**Pros:** Swimming is a fantastic activity for all the family and as island-dwellers I think that it is every parent's duty to ensure their child learns to swim at a young age – leave it too long and your child will be embarrassed that they're going through puberty but sharing lessons with kids who suck their thumb and cry. Armbands are great for older children, but they don't allow for much movement of the arms, which is why the flotation vest is ideal for babies and young children – they can kick with their legs and splash with their hands, but still remain buoyant.

**Cons:** None, other than the fact that I have heard of some public swimming pools that don't allow them, which is a bit odd.

**What's it all about?** Baby flotation jackets are a great way to build your baby's confidence in the water. Checking that the foam blocks are removable when you first decide to buy means that as your toddler becomes more and more familiar with being in a pool, you can start to remove blocks in a surreptitious way to get them to swim with less assistance, or even with no floats at all.

**Bloke's Rating:** A great buy! Now, let's see you try and squeeze into that old pair of Speedos you have at the back of your underpants drawer. Nice.

# Armbands

**Description:** Inflatable bands worn on the arms to keep kids afloat in water.

**Pros:** Armbands are the standard requirement for all kids who will be visiting the pool or beach regularly. They allow your child to float, which will eventually mean that you don't have to be permanently attached to your child for the entire time you're both in the water. Armbands allow kids to kick their legs and move about the pool independently of Dad, without you having to worry about them going too far or what will happen if they venture into a deeper part of the pool.

**Cons:** Don't buy the orange ones or you may have a grumpy pool attendant accusing you of stealing the pool's own supply of armbands.

**What's it all about?** A great way to improve confidence and ability in the water is to inflate the armbands a little less each time you go swimming. Hopefully, before you know it, the armbands will have done their job and your child will be a true water-baby, happy to jump into the pool and paddle around without any additional assistance.

**Bloke's Rating:** An absolute must for the early days in the pool, but as with dummies, your child can become dependant on them. Maybe it's cruel, but we 'forgot' to bring the armbands a few times and this meant our daughter had to get into the water without them.

## Toddler Swimming Floats

**Description:** Condensed foam or rubber shapes which are usually long tubes that your child can hold onto or lie on in the water to aid buoyancy.

**Pros:** The day that your little girl wants to remove her armbands is a proud one for any dad. But just because she doesn't want to wear her armbands, doesn't mean she's actually any good at swimming. Oh, no. What it usually means is that you now have to do the job of the armbands and hold on to your daughter for the entire swim session. Brilliant. A float can help. Your daughter feels more grown-up without her armbands, but is getting the support and the confidence she needs from the float – whilst still looking cool to all the other toddler swimmers. Yes, even little kids like to look cool – and don't pretend you haven't been checking out the other swimmer dads to see who's got the flattest stomach or the biggest arms or the hairiest back.

**Cons:** As the floats aren't actually attached to your child, there can be a bit of a panic when the float slips off, or when another toddler rips it away from your daughter because he wants a go.

**What's it all about?** Baby and toddler pools can be busy places. When you first started bringing your baby to the pool, it would anger you that all these 'big' kids were getting in the way and making far too much noise around your three-month-old child and you were forever being slapped in the face by passing pieces of foam. Now your baby is a few years older and it's your child who is terrorising the newborns and their petrified dads. The circle of life.

**Bloke's Rating:** Yet more clutter for the house and the car; suddenly a simple trip to the pool or the beach is turning into a logistical nightmare, but you'll buy one nonetheless.

## Chemical-Free Mosquito Repellent

**Description:** An electronic device that uses the barely audible sound of a dragonfly's wing-beat to scare off the mozzies. Plug one of these things in and your child should hopefully wake up the next morning without a collection of itchy red marks around her ankles or anywhere else.

**Pros:** Firstly this electronic mosquito repellent is far healthier for your child than using sprays in the room or burning mosquito coils, which are quite repugnant to humans as well as bugs. Mozzie bites are really irritating and if your child is bitten you'll know about it – all day long.

**Cons:** There aren't any guarantees that the repellent will work; one cheeky chappie will always make it through, which sort-of defeats the purpose. The repellent is barely audible but audible nonetheless. The last thing you want or need is to put something in your child's bedroom that's going to keep them awake.

**What's it all about?** Obviously no one is expecting you to holiday in the swamps of Vietnam or India, or Florida for that matter, but there will be times when you want to vacation in southern Europe, or you live near the coast here in the UK where mosquitoes are present. The chemical-free mosquito repellent can indeed keep the mozzies away, but if they're already in the room, it's not going to be an awful lot of help.

**Bloke's Rating:** It's going a bit overboard, really.

## UV Suit

**Description:** UV suits are made from UV50+ rated nylon Lycra and hug the body like a second skin. Some cover the whole body and some cover the torso only. If you're planning to spend a lot of time in your garden with a paddling pool or going on holiday abroad, then you're going to want one of these for your child.

**Pros:** UV suits are pretty groovy – they look like wetsuits or like some of the specialised swimsuits now worn by competitive swimmers – and kids love them. UV suits don't impede movement in the water like a heavy T-shirt can and if you opt for the long-leg version, then your child's legs are protected as well as the chest and back. It'd be a bit unfair and very dangerous to make them wear pyjamas in the pool, and have you ever tried to apply the recommended amount of sun cream to a wriggly, overexcited toddler?

**Cons:** UV suits obviously cost a bit more than a pair of regular swimming trunks, but then you get so much more material for your money. Steer clear of predominantly black material because black soaks up the sun's rays and your child will feel very hot when out of the water.

**What's it all about?** As a child I was lucky enough to go on many a foreign holiday, but the experience was often marred by the fact that after only twenty minutes in the pool, Mum would make my brother and me wear T-shirts. How naff was that? None of the other kids had to wear T-shirts, but then none of the other kids had as many freckles as me, nor did they have a Celtic heritage that meant being burned horrendously by the sun by just looking at it. They were Spanish, olive-skinned and used to it. I was red-raw, had shoulders covered in blisters and I was not used to it, but it was still un-cool to be wearing clothes in the pool. If only UV suits had been around then.

**Bloke's Rating:** Protect and Serve.

## Sun Tent

**Description:** A sun tent is just like a regular tent, only bright red or yellow or green, or even a combination of all three colours. A sun tent is particularly useful when you're planning to spend the whole morning or even the whole day at the beach. Kids need to take a break from the relentless rays of the sun and Baby will need somewhere to nap when everything gets a bit too much. The sun tent also offers the kids a reasonably sand-free area in which to eat their lunch or a snack.

**Pros:** A busy beach can be a nightmare for parents when kids get to the stage where they want to wander around, or play on their own. The sun tent means that your 'camp', which is what it's going to look like, is a beacon for them to keep their eye on when they go off to explore rock pools or other kids' toys. Sun tents are light, so it won't encumber you too much as you march to the sea carrying all that equipment.

**Cons:** Yes, it's just more and more stuff that Dad has to carry over the burning hot sand so that you and your family feel suitably equipped to spend a few hours on the beach. No matter how much you shake the thing, you'll end up carrying a pile of sand back to your house or hotel.

**What's it all about?** It seems so long ago that you could just turn up at the beach with your trunks under your shorts and a towel over your shoulder. One bottle of sun cream between you and the wife and away you go... The sacrifices we make for our kids, even when we're supposed to be taking it easy on holiday.

**Bloke's Rating:** Buy one big enough so that Dad can have a little nap too.

## Tent

**Description:** I doubt that I need to explain what a tent is, but did you know that tent technology has moved on so much in the last ten years that it is now staggering what you can get for your money? It's amazing. £200 ten years ago would buy you a decent two-man dome tent. Now, £200 can buy you at least four to six berths along with a dining room, a 'guest' sleeping quarters and sometimes even free kit, like inflatable mattresses and sleeping bags. Unbelievable. It wasn't so long ago that camping meant six people were trying to get to sleep in the equivalent of a small jiffy bag. Now, for the same money, not only do you get your own compartment or 'room', you get a separate storage area for your boots and pack – how cool is that?

**Pros:** Kids love camping. There are no two ways about it. You might worry about Junior's reaction to the great outdoors, but rest assured, he or she will love it. The fresh air knackers them, the excitement of sleeping in a tent is overwhelming and then there's the bizarre concept that when the sky gets dark there really isn't going to be any more light until tomorrow. Couple all of this with the fact that there is no chance of picking up satellite or cable TV through your torch and it's early nights all round. If only it was so easy back at home.

**Cons:** At first, not every child gets on with camping as well as might be expected and not every parent is as comfortable with the 'risks' of trying it out. Therefore, I advise that your first couple of ventures are to the nearest campsite available – no matter how dreadful or close to home. If you can see your kids taking to the whole experience, then you can always move further afield next time, but for now, practise close to home so that should the whole experience prove to be dreadful, then at least you can get everyone home quickly and easily.

**What's it all about?** Camping is ace. Or at least I think it is and therefore I have forced and will force the experience on my family, whether they like it or not.

**Bloke's Rating:** Get out of the city as often as you can.

# Afterword

Over the course of this book we have looked at the vast array of gadgets currently available for babies and toddlers. Some gadgets you will definitely be able to live without and some you will rely on day after day. There is an awful lot available on the market that is the product of great design and good engineering, offering parents a real help in the day-to-day enjoyment and care of their baby. There are of course a number of manufacturers who have simply tapped into the zeitgeist, or, worse, deliberately play on egos and fears of parents and, with clever marketing and the cooperation of the retailers, convince us that we are bad parents for not buying certain products. At the end of the day the choice is very much yours. There are always going to be products that are absolutely necessary and then there's everything else. If you think twice before rushing into any purchase, you'll probably be all right. Another important thing to remember is that our babies are all unique and therefore what works for one child won't always work for another – even when the children are brother and sister. Over the course of the coming years you will either decide to buy or even be asked to buy certain gadgets, products and toys for your child and they will never get used. This, it seems, is one of the many facets of being a new parent at the turn of the 21st century. Welcome to a very cluttered life full of baby gadgets.

# Useful Contacts

There are both good and bad sources of information available on the Internet. It is important to visit as many sites as possible and to try and get a few different opinions of gadgets before committing to purchase. The Internet is a constantly changing phenomenon and therefore good and bad sites are forever popping up and dropping off. There follows a list, in my opinion, of useful websites, where you can find out more about the products detailed in this book. All links were checked at the time of going to press.

## Online Retailers

http://www.kiddicare.com
http://www.hippychick.co.uk
http://www.nippers.co.uk
http://www.mothercare.com
http://www.babiesrus.co.uk
http://www.babyworld.co.uk
http://www.ebay.co.uk
http://www.amazon.co.uk
http://www.spiritofnature.co.uk

## Online Information

http://www.justdads.co.uk
http://www.babycentre.co.uk
http://www.nfpi.org

http://www.ivillage.co.uk/parenting
http://www.parenting.org.uk
http://www.raisingkids.co.uk
http://www.ukparents.co.uk
http://www.dads-uk.co.uk
http://www.dads-haven.co.uk


## Magazines

*New Baby & Toddler Gear*
*Fathers Quarterly (FQ)*


## Also by Jon Smith:

**For Adults (18-80)**
*The Bloke's Guide to Pregnancy*
*The Bloke's 100 Top Tips for Surviving Pregnancy*
*Websites That Work*
*Smarter Business Start Ups*

**For Children (8-12)**
*Toytopia*

# Words of praise for
# The Bloke's Guide
# to Pregnancy

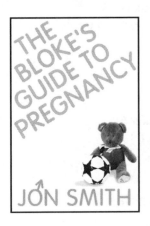

'Excellent advice and information on everything – from options on the type of birth and medical interventions, to being the partner's voice during the birth.' *Relate Magazine*

'Jon Smith gives his lowdown on what men should expect over the happy but stressful nine-month countdown.' *Daily Express*

'Right-on.' *YOU* magazine, *Mail on Sunday*

# Words of praise for
# The Bloke's 100 Top Tips
# for Surviving Pregnancy

100 bite-sized chunks that even the most
book-phobic bloke will be able to digest.

'Easy to digest ... the book covers everything a
first-time father-to-be will want to know about
pregnancy but may be too embarrassed to ask'
*Junior Pregnancy & Baby*

# Hay House Related Titles

*Everything I've Ever Learned About Change*
by Lesley Garner

*How to be a Great Single Dad*
by Theo Theobald

*Pink for a Girl*
by Isla McGuckin

*The Media Diet for Kids*
by Teresa Orange and Louise O'Fynn

*Time Management for Manic Mums*
by Allison Mitchell

*Baby Sign Language Basics*
by Monta Briant

*Sign, Sing, and Play!*
by Monta Briant

We hope you enjoyed this Hay House book.
If you would like to receive a free catalogue featuring additional
Hay House books and products, or if you would like information
about the Hay Foundation, please contact:

## Hay House UK Ltd

292B Kensal Rd • London W10 5BE
Tel: (44) 20 8962 1230; Fax: (44) 20 8962 1239
www.hayhouse.co.uk

\*\*\*

*Published and distributed in the United States of America by:*
Hay House, Inc. • PO Box 5100 • Carlsbad, CA 92018-5100
Tel: (1) 760 431 7695 or (800) 654 5126;
Fax: (1) 760 431 6948 or (800) 650 5115
www.hayhouse.com

*Published and distributed in Australia by:*
Hay House Australia Ltd • 18/36 Ralph St • Alexandria NSW 2015
Tel: (61) 2 9669 4299 • Fax: (61) 2 9669 4144
www.hayhouse.com.au

*Published and distributed in the Republic of South Africa by:*
Hay House SA (Pty) Ltd • PO Box 990 • Witkoppen 2068
Tel/Fax: (27) 11 706 6612 • orders@psdprom.co.za

*Distributed in Canada by:*
Raincoast • 9050 Shaughnessy St • Vancouver, BC V6P 6E5
Tel: (1) 604 323 7100 • Fax: (1) 604 323 2600

\*\*\*

Sign up via the Hay House UK website to receive the Hay House
online newsletter and stay informed about what's going on with
your favourite authors. You'll receive bimonthly announcements
about discounts and offers, special events, product highlights,
free excerpts, giveaways, and more!
**www.hayhouse.co.uk**